ESCAPE FROM
THE DEEP

ESCAPE FROM THE DEEP

*The Epic Story of
a Legendary Submarine and
Her Courageous Crew*

ALEX KERSHAW

Da Capo Press
A Member of the Perseus Books Group

Cataloging-in-Publication Data for this book is available from
the Library of Congress.

ISBN 978-0-306-81519-5

Published by Da Capo Press
A Member of the Perseus Books Group

http://www.dacapopress.com

Da Capo Press books are available at special discounts for bulk purchases in the
U.S. by corporations, institutions, and other organizations. For more information,
please contact the Special Markets Department at the Perseus Books Group,
2300 Chestnut Street, Suite 200, Philadelphia, PA 19103, or call (800) 255-1514,
or email special.markets@perseusbooks.com

2 4 6 8 10 9 7 5 3

For my mother,
in memory of her father, Neville Lee

CONTENTS

ACKNOWLEDGMENTS

There are sadly fewer and fewer survivors from the undersea war in the Pacific, one of the most astonishing success stories in military history. During the writing of this book, two unique American naval officers, who both served in the *Tang*, died. It was my great fortune to meet one of those two men, Murray Frazee. I will always remember his and his wife's hospitality and humor. Mr. Frazee provided extraordinary insight and helped direct my research. The other *Tang* veteran who died during the writing of this book, Larry Savadkin, was just as remarkable. I am indebted to him for talking to me about his harrowing escape from the deep.

Two living survivors of the *Tang*'s final patrol were incredibly helpful. Bill Leibold, the very definition of an officer and a gentleman, was generous with his time. He replied to countless e-mails and spent many hours on the telephone patiently answering questions. His fellow survivor from the *Tang*, Floyd Caverly, was also a most gracious and humorous host, and I enjoyed a couple of afternoons in Oregon with him and his wife. Without the assistance of these two men, this book would have been impossible to write. I cannot thank them enough. It has been an honor to know them and to pay tribute to their fellow submariners of the legendary *Tang*.

I am indebted to a fellow Limey, Leslie Leaney of the Historical Diving Society, for his diligent fact-checking. I was lucky to benefit from Mr. Leaney's and his colleagues at the Historical Diving Society's interest in this book and eleventh hour assistance; Tom Burgess, in particular, read the manuscript with great care and made several key suggestions, as did Nyle Monday at San Jose State University.

The following relatives, veterans, and experts kindly provided help and in many cases spent hours answering my questions, rooting out information, and tracking down photographs and contacts: Joyce DaSilva, widow of Jesse DaSilva; her daughter Joyce Paul, who searched high and low for a great deal of vital documentation; Barbara Lane, sister of Larry Savadkin; Annie Decker, widow of Clay Decker; Marsha Allen, daughter of Dick O'Kane; Jim O'Kane, son of Dick O'Kane; Jackie Morris, daughter of Pete Narowanski; Robin Enos, relative of Mel Enos; Keith Merwin, an expert on Basil Pearce; Ken and Barbara Siegfried, relatives of George Zofcin; Dave Harnish of the U.S. Subvets Western Chapter; John Anderson; Paul Wittmer, a distinguished veteran; and Charles Hinman in Hawaii.

I must also mention the following, all of whom went out of their way to make my job easier: the inimitable broadcaster Rick Crandall in Denver; historian Thomas Saylor in Minnesota; Paul Tullis at Men's Journal; Wendy Gulley, archivist at the Submarine Force Museum in Groton, Connecticut; and George Rocek and Bill Cooper, of the Sculpin, who both experienced all the horrors of imprisonment. The following World War II submarine veterans also provided harrowing testimony about their time as POWs: Thomas Moore, Herbert Thomas, Charles Ver Valin, Kevin Harty, and Ernest Plantz.

· The Indiana Historical Society unearthed wonderful material on Jesse DaSilva, including an oral history that I have quoted at length. Regis University in Colorado was just as generous in sending many hours of invaluable interview material with Clay Decker. The following institutions were also helpful: The Naval Historical Center; the New York Public Library; the University of Minnesota; the Minnesota Historical Society; the museum library at the New London submarine base; Lafayette College; and various chapters of U.S. submarine veterans' associations across the country. I cannot thank the staff at the Sawyer Library at Williams College enough for all their help over the years. They have graciously provided me with a second home during the writing of several books.

The idea for this book was the result of discussions with my editor, Robert Pigeon, of Da Capo Press, and I must thank him yet again for his diligence and dedicated support on this, my fourth book for Da Capo Press. His instincts and loyalty are second to none. My publisher, John Radziewicz, and his colleague Kevin Hanover were just as encouraging. Kate Burke and the best cover designer in book publishing, Alex Camlin, have provided wonderful assistance yet again. Ashley St. Thomas aided me enormously during the editing process, and Christine Marra and Susan Pink did a wonderful job during editorial production and copyediting. I am also grateful to Albert A. Nofi for reading the book and providing comments.

My agent, Derek Johns, and his colleague, Rob Kraitt, and the rest of the team at A. P. Watt in London were also wonderful. Liza Wachter in Los Angeles was an inspiration, as ever. My wife, Robin, and son, Felix, again tolerated my obsessions. I owe them more than I can ever say. My relatives in Britain and in America have also been great supporters.

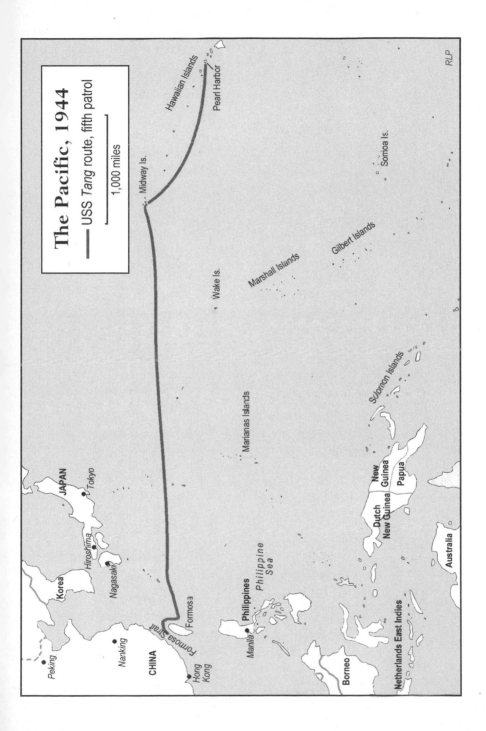

The Pacific, 1944

— USS *Tang* route, fifth patrol

1,000 miles

Hawaiian Islands

Pearl Harbor

Midway Is.

Samoa Is.

Wake Is.

Marshall Islands

Gilbert Islands

Solomon Islands

Marianas Islands

JAPAN

Tokyo

Hiroshima

Nagasaki

Korea

Peking

Nanking

CHINA

Hong Kong

Formosa

Formosa Strait

Philippine Sea

Philippines

Manila

New Guinea

Dutch New Guinea

Papua

Borneo

Netherlands East Indies

Australia

RLP

ESCAPE FROM
THE DEEP

PART ONE

The Last Patrol

It's a big ocean.
You don't have to find the enemy if you don't want to.[1]
—Dick O'Kane

1

Thunder Below

August 11, 1944, a few miles off the coast of Japan

THIRTY-THREE-YEAR-OLD DICK O'KANE peered through a periscope. In the distance, he could see two large Japanese freighters. They would have been easy targets had it not been for the fast-moving gunboats escorting them.

Few submarine captains would have pressed on with their attack. Only the most aggressive, like Commander O'Kane, would contemplate taking them on. Nothing, it seemed, could prevent him from hunting down the enemy. He believed that it was his mission to wage unrestricted warfare on the enemy by sinking vessels small and large—sampans, merchant ships, troop carriers, and Japanese navy ships—as many as he possibly could.

O'Kane switched on the loudspeakers so that his crew of eighty-seven men could listen to his crisp, calm orders. He then prepared to make the approach on the convoy.

Seated in a small cubicle a few yards from O'Kane was twenty-one-year-old Minnesotan Floyd Caverly, known to his fellow submariners as "Friar Tuck." He was listening intently to the sound of the enemy's screws through his headset.

Swish. Swish. Swish. Swish.

The sound reminded the men aboard of a shaving brush being slopped back and forth in a sink.

Caverly looked at a Sherman and Clay Co. metronome in his radio shack. On his last patrol aboard the USS *Tang*, Caverly had begun using it to time the speed of the enemy's screws.

Tick, tock, tick, tock.

O'Kane stood close beside several other officers. They crowded the cramped area of the *Tang*'s conning tower. Their faces were studies in concentration, their features lit up by the small room's eerie red light.

"No change in speed, Captain. Still seven-two turns," reported Caverly.

O'Kane was ready to strike.

"Open all outer doors forward," he ordered. "Stand by for final bearing. Up scope."

Caverly listened carefully, trying to detect any change in the enemy's speed. On his three previous patrols aboard the *Tang*, he had come to trust utterly O'Kane's instincts. The "Old Man" had an innate ability to outwit the enemy—he was a "walking torpedo data computer," able to work out angles and bearings in his head. He had learned his trade from the best, the legendary Dudley "Mush" Morton of the USS *Wahoo*.[2]

Every man depended for his survival right now on Caverly relaying information quickly and accurately. Was the enemy moving toward or away from the *Tang*? What was the enemy's bearing?[3]

Tick, tock, tick, tock

The beat of the enemy's screws was getting faster.

"Fast screws bearing three four zero, Captain," reported Caverly.

O'Kane shifted the periscope quickly and saw a gunboat. It was heading straight for the *Tang*. No part of its bow was exposed, which meant the *Tang* had precious little to aim at. It was closing fast. In less than a minute, it would reach the *Tang*.

O'Kane was undeterred. He decided he still had time to attack the freighters.

"Constant bearing—mark! Keep the sound bearings coming, Caverly."

"Set."

"Fire!"[4]

There were three jolts as three torpedoes were fired in a spread toward a freighter. Another three were soon heading toward another ship.

O'Kane gripped the periscope. He saw his first target explode. But he also saw the Japanese gunboat, still closing fast. It was high time the *Tang* disappeared beneath the waves. He knew he had cut things particularly close.

"Flood negative," ordered O'Kane, trying to sound calm.

"Take her deep," he added. "Rig for depth charge."

The submarine's ballast tanks flooded with fourteen thousand pounds of salt water. She was quickly 180 feet below, close to the sea bottom.

The crew was now sealed off in the *Tang*'s compartments, manning battle stations, rigging the *Tang* for silent running.[5]

"Keep her going down, Larry," O'Kane ordered Lieutenant

Lawrence Savadkin, a quick-witted twenty-four-year-old who had been a track-and-field star at Lafayette College in Pennsylvania before joining the navy.[6]

Floyd Caverly listened to the enemy's screws. They had slowed. The sound of the enemy's sonar echoed inside the *Tang*.

Ping . . . Ping . . . Ping . . .[7]

Sweat beaded Caverly's brow as he tracked the enemy.

Executive Officer Murray Frazee, who was second-in-command of the *Tang*, waited for the inevitable.[8]

"Coming on the range now!" announced one of the crew. "Coming on the range . . . He's dropped the first one!"[9]

The men could hear the splash of a depth charge hitting the water.

Frazee thought about the time he'd spent on a destroyer before volunteering for submarine duty. The depth charges that *he* had dropped on the enemy back then had fallen at around ten feet per second. The *Tang* was now about two hundred feet below the surface.

So in about twenty seconds' time, thought Frazee, *the first explosion will occur . . . if the Japanese have set their charges for the correct depth.*

"He's dropped six of them!" said Caverly.

The slightly balding Caverly looked warily at a pressure gauge located just above his radar. The last time he'd been depth-charged, the *Tang* went down to three hundred feet and the gauge snapped off the bulkhead like a popped shirt button and hit him in the head.[10]

"Ten seconds more, Captain," Frazee announced calmly.[11]

There was a click followed by a sound that felt like "someone hitting the hull with a million sledgehammers." A lightbulb shattered. The *Tang* shook.

Edwin Bergman, the *Tang*'s radioman, screamed and ripped off his headset. He had not turned down the volume and was in agony.

O'Kane grabbed onto the hoist cable of the periscope to steady himself. With a free hand, he propped up Bergman, who was quivering with pain and fear.

Another explosion was followed by another massive vibration, this time upending ashtrays and unsecured objects as the deck plates contorted and shook.

The explosions continued, each one reverberating throughout the submarine, knocking men off their feet.

O'Kane had suffered his fair share of depth charges after ten wartime patrols in two years. But the enemy ship was laying down charges faster and closer than he had ever experienced before.[12]

It was now less than a minute into the attack and the already groggy air was filled with asbestos dust, flecks of paint, and pieces of cork.

It was also the worst depth-charging that twenty-year-old motor mechanic Clayton O. Decker had endured. But he remained composed, struggling to stay upright, standing beside the bow planes in the control room, the nerve center of the submarine.

Decker grew up in the mountains of Colorado, where he had worked as a miner before the war—an ideal qualification in the eyes of his navy recruiter because Decker was unlikely to suffer from claustrophobia after spending so much time so far down.[13] And sure enough, he never did. But the current depth-charging was enough to send even the most hardened veterans like Decker over the edge.[14] It was as if he was "inside an empty fifty-gallon drum with someone beating on it with a hammer."[15]

More explosions. The *Tang* rocked. More lightbulbs popped.

Decker did not know how deep the *Tang* was, but he hoped she was as far down as possible in the short time she had been able to dive. If the *Tang* was below where the charges were exploding, the chance of survival was good. On the other hand, if the *Tang* was too close to the surface, a single explosion below could blow water from the ballast tanks and pop the submarine to the surface like a cork.

The enemy's sonar could detect even the faintest noise from the submarine. Everything that could make a sound had been shut off, including the air-conditioning. As soon as its cool breeze had disappeared, intense heat from the engines and motors had started to spread through the *Tang*. Sweat now ran off the men in a constant stream.[16]

In the conning tower, Captain O'Kane and Executive Officer Frazee exchanged anxious glances. The *Tang* was made of stern stuff. But how much more pounding could she take?

Bergman, the sound man, returned to his post in the sound shack, his ears still ringing. He put on his headphones again and heard the enemy's screws once more.

The Japanese were now on the *Tang*'s port bow and slowing down, perhaps waiting to see if the depth-charging had been successful before dropping another round of "ash cans."

O'Kane spoke into the conning tower's telephone: "Check and report all compartments!"[17]

It didn't take long for O'Kane to hear back. By some miracle, there had been no serious damage.

"She's turning this way," said Bergman.

The crew braced themselves for more explosions.

"Here she comes!"

"Shifting to short scale!"

"Screws speeding up!"

"Right full rudder!" ordered O'Kane. "All ahead full!"[18]

So far, the *Tang* had been moving at "evasive speed"—as slow as possible—and with only the slightest noise. "All ahead full" meant no more silent running. The Japanese were bound to detect the *Tang*. Nevertheless, that is what O'Kane ordered and soon the *Tang* was turning toward her tormentor—the gunboat. Incredibly, in the next few seconds, she snuck right under the Japanese boat. The captain of the Japanese boat was no fool, however, and quickly ordered the dropping of another volley of charges.

There were sixteen in all. They exploded in a "prolonged, unpunctuated, smashing, shattering cataclysm."[19] It was a heart-stopping experience: Deck plates lifted as men were thrown about and everything in the submarine seemed to shake. The vibration became so intense that men clutching wheels shivered as if they were being electrocuted. The electrician's mates were similarly affected as they held down levers and switches, grateful that they were at least wearing protective asbestos gloves.

In the conning tower, O'Kane and Frazee somehow stayed on their feet. It would surely be only a few seconds before the *Tang* took a fatal hit. It was hard to believe that she was still operable at all.

A long silence passed. The depth-charging was over.

The *Tang* continued at full speed toward deeper water, away from the coast, and the Japanese gunboat was soon left far behind, vainly searching for wreckage. One of the crew made a tally. There had been twenty-two very close detonations.

Men opened the doors sealing each compartment and began to move through the boat, nerves jangled, hugely relieved that the worst depth-charging any of them had experienced was over.

O'Kane went to the officer's dining room, joining Frazee and a shocked Larry Savadkin.

"Captain," said Savadkin, "if I had known that depth charges would be like those, I might have stayed in surface ships."

"They seemed close because you're not used to them," replied

O'Kane. "When we get some that are really close, these won't seem too bad."

Frazee was noticeably quiet.

O'Kane laughed to break the tension and then conceded that the experience had also rattled him to the core. Were it not for her extra-thick hull, the *Tang* might well be on the bottom, lost with all hands.

Savadkin pulled out the boat's well-worn cribbage board as Frazee left to go check on every compartment and assess the damage. Before long, he reported back that the damage had been mercifully light given the intensity of the attack—several smashed lightbulbs but little else.[20]

Although uninjured, the crew looked badly shaken.[21] They needed a good shot of brandy to calm their nerves. Frazee returned to the conning tower and made a drinking motion, indicating to O'Kane that it was time to distribute the so-called "depth-charge medicine." O'Kane readily agreed.

Frazee had counted every depth charge he had ever heard— about 250 had been dropped during his first ten patrols. On this, his eleventh, he reckoned there had been 250 more.[22]

SEVERAL DAYS LATER, the *Tang* was heading back to Pearl Harbor. O'Kane announced, to the crew's delight, that there would be no stopping in Midway to refuel. Nor would they waste time practicing a daily trim dive. It had been a short but highly effective fourth patrol, and O'Kane was eager to return to base, load up with more "fish"—torpedoes—and get back to sinking the enemy.

As the *Tang* slowly pulled away from Japanese waters, the men began to unwind. When not busy cleaning and preparing for a refit, they gorged themselves on steaks and ice cream—the submarine service was rightly famous for the finest chow in the military. O'Kane ordered that whatever steak they could not finish on the patrol be cut up and served at a shore party when the *Tang* got back to Hawaii.

For three more days the *Tang* was within range of Japanese antisubmarine planes, but O'Kane still opted to run on the surface, with extra lookouts, to save time.[23]

Murray Frazee was far from happy as he navigated the *Tang* toward Pearl Harbor. He was feeling "jittery" after so many patrols—eleven in total now, more than any other submariner he knew. "Twenty-two percent of all those who made war patrols were lost, in fifty-two submarines," he would later write. "I think I deserved to be a little [nervous] by my eleventh patrol, especially operating with Dick O'Kane."[24]

Frazee was uncomfortable with the risks that O'Kane was taking, seemingly as a matter of routine. He was in command of several inexperienced officers. More and more, he wondered whether they could cope if the submarine was surprised on the surface. Along with his chief quartermaster, Sidney Jones, Frazee felt he had no option but to stay awake every night on the return so he could be on hand should anything go wrong.[25] Only when he could actually see Pearl Harbor would he be able to relax.[26]

The *Tang* finally entered Pearl Harbor. As was customary, the chief quartermaster, Jones, went to a locker under the chart desk in the conning tower and pulled out the battle flag. He then climbed to the bridge of the submarine and raised the flag until it fluttered for all to see. It was covered with small Japanese flags, each one indicating a record haul in enemy ships in just the eight months that the *Tang* had been at war.

At the center of the flag was a black panther, one of the most elegant predators in the animal kingdom. "It was determined that we should be known as the 'Black Panther of the Pacific,'" recalled Bill Leibold, the *Tang*'s chief boatswain's mate. "The flag was to reflect this theme. We were fortunate in having an aspiring artist on board, one John Kassube, who actually designed our flag (with a great deal of input from all hands). The flag was basically a copy of the Japanese man of war, with a black panther jumping through the large red ball, Meatball as we called it. Sidney Jones fabricated the flag with signal bunting, using our portable Singer sewing machine."[27]

O'Kane did the usual rounds as the patrol came to an end, inspecting the compartments. In the pump room he was surprised to find a purple stain on a pipe. For several days, Floyd Caverly had frantically tried to get rid of the stain. It had appeared because of a leak from a homemade still that he had secretly installed in the *Tang*. On this patrol the still was producing a powerful hooch made from purple Welch's grape juice.[28] Thankfully, O'Kane did not inquire about the stain's source.

A few miles from Pearl Harbor, O'Kane was standing on the bridge when he noticed two other submarines behind the *Tang*, also making for the submarine base there.

One of the subs, the USS *Rasher,* signaled with a light: FORM ONE EIGHT. This meant that the *Tang* was to fall in astern of the signaling boat, which would then enter Pearl Harbor first. The signal was sent by Captain Hank Munson, a brilliant mathematician and Rhodes scholar, who was completing what would turn out to be the second greatest patrol of the Pacific War in terms of tonnage sunk.

Munson was wearing a freshly pressed khaki uniform with a black tie. Above him fluttered a hand-sewn battle flag. His crew was lined up at quarters on the deck before him, as eager as their captain to be the first to reach the ten-ten dock in Pearl Harbor, where successful submarines berthed after grueling patrols. The entire *Rasher* crew deserved to be first after sinking four large ships and an escort carrier. Munson had seniority as a full commander with two navy crosses to his name. By rights, certainly in peacetime, it was his role to lead the submarines back to harbor.

O'Kane turned to his signalman, Edwin Ogden, and told him to pretend that he didn't understand the command. The following messages then came from the *Tang*: IMI (repeat) and INT (I don't understand) as Chief Electrician James Culp took the *Tang* to full power and left Munson fuming, far behind in the *Tang*'s wake.

Munson was later said to be outraged by O'Kane's insubordination and arrogance. But O'Kane couldn't have cared less as the *Tang* pulled up to the prized ten-ten dock ahead of Munson. He was not the type to be upstaged by any man, certainly not a competing submariner, no matter how brilliant.

2

The Bravest Man

TWENTY-ONE-YEAR-OLD CLAY DECKER lined up with his fellow crew members on the deck as the *Tang* neared the ten-ten dock in Pearl Harbor.[1] Like the other noncommissioned men, he sported freshly laundered dungarees and a white hat. He could see Vice Admiral Charles Lockwood, O'Kane's commanding officer, standing on the dock beside other submarine big chiefs, waiting to greet the *Tang*.[2]

The submarine base's band played as fifty-four-year-old Lockwood, nicknamed "Uncle Charlie," welcomed his favorite captain back to American soil and congratulated him on another outstanding patrol. A quick-thinking, incisive leader, Lockwood genuinely cared about his men and they knew it. No man was as experienced in submarine fleet command, none understood more what war beneath the waves truly entailed. Lockwood had cap-tained seven submarines, dating back to the gas-powered pig boats of World War I, before becoming commander of Submarine Force, Pacific Fleet (ComSubPac).

Like the other men in dungarees, some sallow faced, others with deep tans because of their lookout duties, Decker relished every moment of every return to base. In a few minutes, he would be able to gorge on fresh oranges and bananas—it was customary to welcome returning crews with such wartime delicacies. Mail from his attractive young wife, Lucille, back in San Francisco, might be waiting on the dockside. Once he caught up on news about her and his two-year-old son, he could get drunk and enjoy fifteen days of R and R at the swank 425-room Royal Hawaiian Hotel.[3]

Decker was planning to get one of the better rooms at the ho-tel, featuring large lanais that overlooked the beach and Diamond Head; maybe he would get the very suite where none other than movie star Mae West had slept before the war. Before long, Decker would take his first proper shower in weeks, letting the cold, fresh water splash on his head. That night, he would sleep like a baby on a clean, soft bed that did not move at night. He would not have to lie flat on his back to keep from rolling out. He could sleep in until the sun swung past Diamond Head and spilled through the big windows.

For several days, Decker and his fellow crew members ate fresh food and sunbathed.[4] Dick O'Kane, however, had little rest other than an afternoon swimming and surfing on a long board. He was busy overseeing the *Tang's* refit and attending briefings on the progress of the war. He also had the sad task of signing the offi-cial transfer for his right-hand man, Murray Frazee, who, after four patrols with the *Tang,* was leaving the submarine, much to O'Kane's regret. "We had been through much this past year," O'Kane would later write, "and with results that neither of us could have accomplished without the other. The skipper-exec was a unique relationship in submarines but I was . . . blessed."[5]

The *Tang's* new executive officer was twenty-six-year-old Frank Springer, a highly capable lieutenant whom O'Kane had groomed for command through four remarkable patrols. Tall and lean, Springer had graduated top of his class in submarine school. He made his home with his young wife, Carolyn, in Huntington Park, California. When he joined the *Tang,* crewmates considered him to be a rather humorless, serious-faced torpedo officer.

With men like Springer helping out, the turnabout for the *Tang* was completed in record time. Barely three weeks after returning from the fourth patrol, O'Kane and his crew were ready to set out on their fifth patrol, proud in the knowledge that the *Tang* was now officially the deadliest submarine operating in the Pacific.

O'Kane himself was the most successful captain among Vice Admiral Lockwood's so-called "underwater aces," having sunk more ships than any other captain in just four patrols. He and his crew had also been involved in some of the more dramatic incidents of the submarine war in the Pacific, from the rescue of twenty-two downed aviators on the second patrol, to the sinking of a record ten merchant ships, totaling more than thirty-nine thousand tons, on her third outing. All this had been achieved in less than a year since the *Tang's* commissioning on October 15, 1943, in Mare Island.

RICHARD HETHERINGTON O'KANE was a unique commander, a true maverick in Murray Frazee's eyes. "Never was there such an aggressive submarine officer as Dick O'Kane," recalled Frazee. "In fact, there were some who doubted his sanity, at times, in pushing to get the *Tang* out to sea and in contact with the enemy."[6]

If O'Kane had any antecedents with which to compare, they would have been the freewheeling frigate captains of John Paul Jones's early American navy, piratical master sailors who understood that a raider is at his best when destroying commercial boats in bold, hit-and-run attacks.

Born in Dover, New Hampshire, the son of an entomology professor at the University of New Hampshire, O'Kane was raised with the smell of saltwater always in the air. He was the youngest of four children, all of them Irish to the core. A keen sailor as a boy, he was also academically gifted and won a partial scholarship to an elite prep school, Phillips Academy in Andover. At Phillips, he received a classical education—to the end of his life he would be able to recite Latin phrases, French poems, verses from Coleridge's *The Ancient Mariner*, and some of Robert Frost's most popular lines.[7] He was notable for being one of very few students who yearned for a navy career.

At age nineteen, O'Kane gained entry to the Naval Academy in Annapolis, where he graduated 264th in his class of 464 midshipmen in 1934. The academy's yearbook noted that O'Kane was an elegant dancer, popular with the ladies, a first-class skier and tennis player, and a "Yankee and proud of it."[8]

O'Kane first served on a heavy cruiser, the USS *Chester,* and then for two long years on an old four-stack destroyer, the USS *Pruitt.* During an overhaul in Mare Island in June 1936, O'Kane married a petite young woman named Ernestine Groves, whom he had first met as a young boy in Durham; until O'Kane had been nine years old, the two had in fact been neighbors. Ernestine was also the child of an academic at the University of New Hampshire.

O'Kane opted for Submarine School in New London, Connecticut, where he spent six months working his hardest, knowing that the top third of his class would automatically be assigned to active submarine duty. Among his peers was Slade Cutter, a brilliant football star, destined like O'Kane to be one of World War II's finest captains. O'Kane graduated in the top ten of his class and began his submarine service on the USS *Argonaut*, the largest submarine in the U.S. Navy at the time, designed as a mine-layer.

The *Tang's* twenty-one-year-old chief boatswain's mate, Bill Leibold, a hard-driving California native, had also served on the *Pruitt* before joining the *Tang* for her first patrol. "O'Kane had established a reputation because he had been the executive officer on the *Wahoo* with 'Mush' Morton," he recalled. "Everybody knew about Morton and the *Wahoo*. Morton was a legend, the most talked about submarine captain."[9]

In fact the entire Silent Service knew of the big-fisted, Dudley "Mush" Morton and his brilliant sidekick, Dick O'Kane. Both were said to be equally obsessed with sinking enemy ships. Together, they had reinvented the rules of submarine combat, taking the war to the enemy's front porch during their five patrols together.

Before they devised these new submarine combat techniques, the navy had used a standard procedure for attack. As Leibold explained, "A submarine was to stay submerged, not to be seen. It would fire from periscope depth, not when surfaced. There was even an assigned speed of approach. It was all cut and dried in the official manual. Then along came Mush Morton, who just ignored it. He told O'Kane: 'Your job is to trail that ship and I'll maneuver the boat, and we'll do it from the surface . . . I don't give a damn if it is daylight or pitch dark.' The enemy was never looking for you on the surface. Morton and O'Kane took advantage of this. The brass back in Pearl would say: 'They can't do this! What the hell is going on?' But Morton came back with record numbers of ships sunk. It was no wonder—he damn near sunk himself."[10]

Before the *Tang*'s first patrol, O'Kane had gathered his men and repeated Mush Morton's maxim: "It is our job to sink as many boats as possible. That's how we can get the war over with as soon as possible."[11] O'Kane had also made it clear that he would require every man to give his all, but in return he would make life as comfortable as possible for them when they were not sending enemy shipping to the bottom. And sure enough, he was a man of his word, managing to get hold of an ice-cream maker and baking oven for the *Tang*.[12] Steak and fries followed by fresh vanilla ice cream and baked hot apple pie would be standard fare aboard the *Tang*. Whatever he could wheedle, O'Kane obtained—whether it was fresh fruit for the mess or the latest radar and sonar technology for the crew in the conning tower.

Before going to sea, the *Tang* was arguably the best equipped, best stocked, most up-to-date Balao-class diesel electric submarine in the Pacific: a superlative fighting machine, capable of over twenty knots when surfaced, almost nine when submerged, powered by four state-of-the-art Fairbanks-Morse pistol diesel engines, and armed with twenty-four Mark 18 torpedoes carrying 565 pounds of Torpex high explosives.

O'Kane had cut no corners in preparing his new boat and crew for combat, pushing both to the limit. He knew that the Japanese were becoming more and more skilled in antisubmarine techniques. Indeed, they had caught up fast. Until 1943, they had been ineffective on the whole in combating U.S. submarines. The depth charges they had used had not been as powerful as American ones and had been set to explode only at depths above 150 feet. This meant that as long as boats went to 300 feet during evasion, they stood little chance of being sunk by a depth charge.

It was a closely guarded secret that had saved many lives—the kind of intelligence that reinforced the Silent Service's determination to keep quiet about its activities. "We operated under such secrecy and anonymity," explained Vice Admiral Lockwood, "that only the barest mention was made of these men of lonely heroism, who fought the war not in the newspaper headlines but sealed off beneath the sea, in great steel hulls that sometimes became their tombs. We preferred to publish nothing at all, not even the score of enemy ships sunk by returning submarines. We wanted no part of the Navy Department's campaign for play-by-play account of the war. We wanted the Japanese to think their existing methods were highly effective, that another of our subs had gone to Davy Jones's locker."[13]

Only rarely were the press allowed anywhere near a submarine captain, and then it was only for propaganda purposes: By 1944, the American public had largely forgotten that after Pearl Harbor, although three aircraft carriers had survived the attack, the submarines were the last line of defense—all that had prevented the Japanese from gaining mastery of the Pacific.

Every so often, now that the tide had turned in favor of the Americans, a well-placed story about a submarine's thrilling exploits helped remind those who had forgotten about the Silent Service. What the public didn't know was that the Silent Service was now sinking more than half of all Japanese ships—more than the Army's air forces and the U.S. Navy's surface ships and carrier planes combined.

As far as submariners were concerned, the publicity mattered little. Staying alive concerned them far more. By 1944, every man in the service had friends who were "missing in action," on eternal patrol. The all-volunteer force suffered the highest mortality rate of all the armed services. There were few casualties. Unlike a surface ship, when a submarine was sunk no one was expected to return.[14]

THE SILENT SERVICE'S greatest single injury in World War II was inflicted not by the enemy, but by a politician. In 1943, sixty-eight-year-old Congressman Andrew Jackson May, a member of the House Military Affairs Committee, held a press conference and mentioned the unmentionable—Japanese claims of submarine sinkings were way too high because they set their depth charges to go off at too shallow a depth.

His statement outraged every submariner in the service. It was an amazing breach of security, unrivaled during the war. And it didn't take long for the Japanese navy to learn of it through newspaper reports, and then quickly adjust its depth-charge settings accordingly. Lockwood was furious. "I hear Congressman May said the depth charges are not set deep enough," he explained in a letter dripping with sarcasm. "He would be pleased to know [the Japanese] set them deeper now." Later, Lockwood stated: "I consider that indiscretion cost us ten submarines and eight hundred officers and men."[15]

To O'Kane and the other submarine captains, it was soon clear that the Japanese were dropping their charges at the right depth and with greater accuracy. They knew that the near-deadly experience of the USS *Puffer* on its first patrol in October 1943 provided more than enough evidence of the effects of May's treasonable stupidity. For nearly thirty-eight hours, at 500 feet below, the *Puffer's* crew had been pounded by a terrier-like Japanese sub-chaser.

Men became so dehydrated in the pressure-cooker-like conditions that they could not replenish their body fluids and vomited everything they drank. When they stepped from the maneuvering room, where the thermometer showed 125 degrees, to the after-torpedo room, where it was a relatively cool 100 degrees, their bodies seemed to turn to jelly, wracked by shivering and maddening chills.[16]

O'Kane learned all about the *Puffer*'s terrifying experience from a report issued to captains that gave a blow-by-blow account of the ordeal.[17] At 500 feet, the *Puffer* had barely managed to survive. The lesson was obvious to O'Kane: The *Tang* and her crew needed to be able to dive as fast as possible and stay as deep as possible if they were going to stand a chance against an ever more accurate and deadly enemy. During practice dives, O'Kane worked his crew hard, pushing them to the edge, until the *Tang* was able to plunge from the surface to periscope depth—some 60 feet below—in just thirty seconds.

Then, wanting to know what would happen at unprecedented depths, O'Kane ordered the *Tang* down to far beyond her specified test depth of 300 feet. At 450 feet, the *Tang* started to rebel. A gauge line broke and a hose burst. Thankfully, a quick-witted crewmember jammed a raw potato into the line to stop the leak and crisis was averted. At 525 feet, however, there was more significant damage, forcing the *Tang* to surface for repairs.

The next day, O'Kane took the *Tang* even deeper. The old hands were astonished when she reached 580 feet. This time, a vent sprang a leak. Again, the boat surfaced for repairs. It seemed as if O'Kane had a death wish: The very next day, at first light, he ordered his crew to take the *Tang* back down, deeper than before. Soon, the needle on the depth gauge pointed beyond 575 feet. Then it reached the 600-foot mark. It would not record any deeper. Still the *Tang* continued inexorably down. No U.S. submarine had ever ventured so far from the surface. O'Kane asked one of his officers to hold her level.[18] While several crew members struggled to stay calm, the *Tang* maneuvered back and forth with ease, her thick hull resisting the incredible sea pressure of nineteen tons per square foot.

The *Tang* was able to take it, but the same could not be said for all of the crew. One of the old hands aboard, a chief cook named Marvin E. Breedlove, was convinced that O'Kane was going to get them all killed—he was some modern-day Ahab, a reckless buccaneer obsessed with sinking "Nips."

After docking, the sturdily built Breedlove approached wiry bantam-weight Murray Frazee and angrily demanded a transfer. Frazee said that was not possible—the cook would have to complete at least one patrol before being granted a transfer.[19]

"Well, if you're not going to do anything about it now, I just won't show up tomorrow morning."

Frazee, capable of ruthless efficiency and used to playing the role of bad cop for O'Kane, turned to another grizzled veteran, Chief Torpedoman's Mate William Ballinger, who was also chief of the boat, and said: "Chief, you heard what he said, didn't you?"

"I sure did!"

Frazee grabbed the cook's shirt and yanked him so he was close to his face.

"Listen, you son of a bitch, if you're not here tomorrow morning at 0800 when we sail, I'm going to have you tried for desertion in time of war and get you shot! Now, have you got that straight?"[20]

The cook left the *Tang* after her first patrol.

Three patrols and six months later, the *Tang*'s crew had had plenty of opportunities to see O'Kane in action. There were no longer any doubters. O'Kane's men had come to respect and trust him like no other captain they had known.

The bond was special, for a submarine skipper has absolute power over life and death, far more so than the commander of a surface ship. The wrong decision at 600 feet below could be fatal. An error in a frigate might, at worst, mean taking to a lifeboat. "O'Kane was very calculating, brilliant, and very aggressive—too much so for some of the crew," explained Bill Leibold. "But they all said if they had to go to war with any captain, it would be O'Kane."[21]

DICK O'KANE WATCHED as a refit crew attended to the *Tang*. He could see them scurrying about the *Tang's* decks, loading torpedoes, readying her for the next patrol. It was Wednesday, September 20, 1944, a beautiful fall day in Pearl Harbor.

A Jeep pulled up at the dockside.

The driver said he had an urgent message for O'Kane: Vice Admiral Lockwood wanted to see O'Kane immediately.

A tanned and fit O'Kane was soon seated in Lockwood's office. There were the usual pleasantries and good humor. Then the always energetic Lockwood, with three stars on his shirt collar, got down to business. He would not normally provide his skippers with a choice of missions, but O'Kane had to be handled with more finesse than the others. Lockwood laid out the alternatives: join a wolf pack or operate alone in the Pacific's most dangerous waters—the Formosa Strait, between Formosa and mainland China.

The Formosa Strait was strewn with extensive minefields and ploughed by Japanese antisubmarine patrols that continued around the clock.[22] "Offering little room for ships to maneuver," recalled O'Kane, "the strait was an ideal place for submarines to lurk in ambush; the great bulk of Japanese shipping passed through here on the way to and from the South China Sea. Unfortunately for the Americans, however, the enemy held the coasts on both sides of the strait, making it as perilous for the hunters as the hunted."[23]

In four patrols, O'Kane had already sunk seventeen ships for a total of eighty-two thousand tons. He was hungry for more. There was no question that he would go it alone and head for the Formosa Strait, the last hot spot in the Pacific undersea war.

"How soon could you be ready to head west? All the way west?" asked Lockwood.

"Four days sir," replied O'Kane. "But there is one thing I request in return."

"Yes?"

"Admiral, the *Tang* has been banging out patrols at nearly twice the customary rate. Most have been short, but so has every upkeep. My boat needs an ST scope [radar periscope], and I need something to take back to my crew. I'd like our next upkeep scheduled for Mare Island."

Returning to Mare Island in San Francisco Bay would mean the crew could reconnect with their families during extensive shore leave.

"I appreciate what you say," said Lockwood, "and I'll take care of it."

Lockwood and O'Kane shook hands.

O'Kane then called his crew together. Ever anxious to return to combat, he had already cut the *Tang*'s period in dry dock short by four days, irritating some of them.[24] To cushion the blow, O'Kane told his men that after this next patrol they would have an extended furlough on the U.S. mainland: The *Tang* would need a major overhaul and it would last at least six weeks in sunny California.

O'Kane then broke the news that he had volunteered the *Tang* for the toughest assignment possible. He could not tell them where they were going until they left Pearl Harbor. But he could say one thing for sure: There would be good hunting. And the risks would be worth it if they managed to sink several ships.

It was customary in the Silent Service to allow any man who requested a transfer to do so without fear of being punished or stigmatized. Now was the time for any doubters to leave. None did.

Floyd Caverly later recalled the crew's reaction to O'Kane's news that they were embarking on their most hazardous mission to date: "We knew that we were going into very dangerous waters. We knew it would be tough. But we also knew we were going to the only place where there was good hunting. O'Kane warned us that anything could happen out there. We were within aircraft range, destroyer range . . . It was hot territory. But where else would we want to go?"[25]

Dick O'Kane, like his boat and his crew, was also long overdue for a rest, having served under Morton and then completing four patrols with the *Tang*. He knew it and so did the top brass; the commander of the submarine fleet, Vice Admiral Lockwood, did not want his captains to burn out with fatal results. This next patrol might be O'Kane's last of the war, so he was determined to go out with a series of mighty bangs, making it his best patrol. He was already confident that once the navy had awarded his men medals for their fourth patrol, the *Tang* would be the most decorated U.S. submarine in the Pacific.[26] On her fifth patrol, probably his last as her skipper, the *Tang* would, he hoped, seal her record as the greatest U.S. submarine of the entire war.

3

The Most Dangerous Mission

DICK O'KANE STOOD on the bridge of the *Tang*, watching as final supplies and the last of the submarine's twenty-four torpedoes were brought aboard.[1] Hoses and power lines snaked along the *Tang*'s deck and then sagged across the few feet separating her from the dock. There was a sudden flurry of activity on the dockside as Fleet Admiral Nimitz and Vice Admiral Lockwood arrived with an impressive entourage. A few minutes later, they began to award the *Tang*'s crew their medals for the third patrol.[2]

O'Kane received a second Navy Cross. Silver Stars went to Chief Quartermaster Sidney Jones, Frank Springer, the newly promoted executive officer who had replaced Frazee, and Lieutenant Hank Flanagan. Radio Technician's Mate Floyd Caverly got a Bronze Star. "These presentations were not all, however," recalled O'Kane, "for more important than any one or all of them combined was the award of the Presidential Unit Citation. Signed by Franklin D. Roosevelt, it cited the actions during the *Tang*'s first three patrols, and from that moment every man who served in the *Tang* would wear the ribbon with its blue, gold, and red horizontal stripes, and with a star if aboard during the actions cited. I believed our boat now led all others in personal and unit awards. In any case, no submarine captain could have been prouder of his fighting ship and men."[3]

Before the *Tang* left the dock, Vice Admiral Lockwood boarded and drank coffee with O'Kane in his stateroom. The coffee was served by the *Tang*'s steward's mate, Howard Walker, one of only two black men on board. A chronic gambler, this Kentucky native was lucky to still be on the *Tang*. At the beginning of the previous patrol, he held up the submarine's departure because he had lost track of time during a marathon craps game.[4]

According to Caverly, Walker was not court-martialed for this, or for many other lapses, because O'Kane had come to depend on him so much. "Walker really catered to the officers. The Old Man's shoes were always polished. His clothes were always folded and his shirts beautifully ironed—most of the officers couldn't iron a dish rag."[5]

That morning, Walker brewed the coffee to perfection. O'Kane and Lockwood sipped it in the captain's cabin for several minutes as they discussed the progress of the war. Their conversation was interrupted by the sound of the *Tang*'s diesels firing up. Lockwood and O'Kane climbed up to the bridge, shook hands, and then Lockwood stepped ashore.

As the *Tang* announced her departure with a five-second blast from her Klaxons, Lockwood and other base personnel stood at attention.[6]

"All back two-thirds," ordered O'Kane.

The *Tang*'s diesel engines roared.

"Left twenty degrees rudder . . . All ahead two-thirds, shift the rudder."

It was one o'clock on September 24 as the *Tang* left the dockside, headed for the Formosa Strait via Midway at four-engine power.[7] The harbor was much as it had been before the attack on December 7, 1941.[8] Most of the ships stricken that day had been moved, with the notable exception of the USS *Arizona*.

O'Kane looked around and remembered how he had felt when he returned from a patrol in late January 1942. He had been greeted by scenes of utter devastation along so-called battleship row. He and the men lined up on the deck of the USS *Argonaut* had cried unashamedly.

To his port and starboard, O'Kane spotted the red and black channel buoys that guided his boat out of the harbor. In the distance, he could see the sea buoy that marked the true starting location of the *Tang*'s fifth patrol.[9]

Finally, the *Tang* cleared the submarine nets around Pearl Harbor. As was customary, O'Kane then went to his cabin, unlocked the safe, and opened his formal orders.

Not long after, he informed the crew of where they were headed. "We discovered that we were going to be on patrol in the Formosa Strait," recalled Clay Decker. "It was a hot area. We knew we would see action."[10]

All went smoothly at first. Three days after leaving Pearl Harbor, the *Tang* approached Midway. The prospect of a brief liberty on the island, however, brought little excitement among the crew.

In Floyd Caverly's eyes, it was "nothing but a sand-spit with a bunch of gooney birds on it. That was about it." The men would sometimes play drunken volleyball there if they had time, but otherwise it was not the kind of stopover they wrote home about, unlike Perth in Australia or their favorite port for a spot of liberty, San Francisco.[11]

O'Kane had a choice: He could either bypass Midway and forgo topping up the *Tang*'s diesel tanks or enter a north-facing narrow channel in choppy seas with the wind blowing from the south, a difficult maneuver. O'Kane opted for extra fuel, but as he entered the channel he began to have second thoughts. The *Tang* began to yaw alarmingly. Anxious moments followed. With only yards to spare, O'Kane managed to avoid running the *Tang* aground, steering her through a narrow gap in the reef.[12]

It was seven o'clock in the morning on September 27, 1944, when the *Tang* moored at the submarine base in Midway. Two new young officers came aboard: twenty-four-year-old Lieutenant Paul Wines, an outstanding athlete and scholar who had been president of his high school's student council in Ridgewood, New Jersey, and Lieutenant John Heubeck, who grew up in Baltimore, where he had won several awards for swimming.[13]

With her tanks topped up, the *Tang* left after just five hours at Midway with two of her four engines operating, and was soon bucking through heavy seas in increasingly stormy weather, headed for Formosa.[14] The *Tang*'s recently departed executive officer, Murray Frazee, would later write that O'Kane was always in a hurry to get to Midway "just so he could load up more torpedoes and get back out there—sink more ships, kill more Japs."[15]

O'Kane wanted to reach Formosa before a planned air strike on the island so he could stand by, ready to pick up any downed aviators. But he made slow headway in the eight-foot waves at two-engine speed. Three days after leaving Midway, however, the storm abated for a while and O'Kane added a third engine, hoping to make up for lost time. There were some practice dives as the *Tang* continued west; O'Kane was delighted by the crew's speed and efficiency.

On October 4, the *Tang* received a coded message—a wolf pack comprised of the USS *Trigger* and the USS *Sunfish* was looking for a small Japanese weather ship. The ship's last reported position was right in the track of the *Tang*. It seemed that the wolf pack was trailing the *Tang*, even though its boats had left Pearl Harbor first. O'Kane felt he had a good chance of finding the enemy ship first, especially if the codebreakers back in Hawaii were on their usual game.[16]

Throughout the war, O'Kane and his fellow captains had been aided immeasurably by the genius of American cryptographers in breaking Japanese naval codes. By this stage of the war, it was not unusual on any one day for all but a handful of American submarines on patrol in the central Pacific to be operating on instructions derived from the prompt breaking of Japanese codes.[17]

On October 6, the weather worsened significantly.[18] Among the first to feel the effects was Floyd Caverly, who had been an amateur boxer before the war. Although he was used to being knocked around in the ring, he was particularly sensitive to increased pitching and rolling. In fact, Caverly's stomach had become as accurate as a barometer: When Caverly started to puke, a storm never failed to materialize. "The [crew] got me a little piss pot with a handle on it," he recalled, "and I was supposed to hook that onto my belt so I had something to heave into. It was a big joke. The slow rolls didn't bother me too much. It was the pitch."[19]

O'Kane called an inspection for midmorning to make sure the *Tang* was ready to weather a storm. At the assigned time, he began his inspection in the forward engine room, where he found, among others, his junior officers gathered in a group: Hank Flanagan, Ed Beaumont, Mel Enos, Dick Kroth, John Heubeck, Paul Wines, and Basil Pearce. Only one of them was destined to survive the patrol.

Addressing his captain, Frank Springer explained why he assembled the group, "I suggested that they be here to see what you demand on these inspections."

The *Tang*'s officers saluted.

O'Kane returned their salute, stepped forward, and suddenly fell through the deck to the engine room five feet below. Someone had left a hatch open. O'Kane landed on the bottom rung of a ladder, breaking his left foot. Doubled up in agony, sick with pain, he began to sweat heavily.[20] His men helped him up and he limped to his cabin, where Pharmacist's Mate Paul "Doc" Larson examined his foot.

Larson gave his captain a painkiller and set his foot before bandaging it. O'Kane would have to hobble around for a few days "like a three-legged dog."[21]

"You've got some small broken bones, Captain," said Larson. "I can feel them but they're pretty straight now—and one hell of a sprain. There's nothing they'd do ashore that I haven't done except to take some X-rays, and I already know about what they'd look like."[22]

O'Kane lay on his bunk, his foot propped up on the gray bulkhead and his ear next to the intercom, bitching mightily and listening to the wind howling and waves slapping against the *Tang*. There was no question of letting up for even a few hours: Frank Springer took over the running of the boat from the conning tower while O'Kane issued commands over the intercom, or "squawk box."[23]

The weather continued to deteriorate rapidly, waves doubling in size every hour. O'Kane ordered the lookouts to come below, leaving senior watch officer Larry Savadkin alone on the bridge. Angry green waves now pounded against the *Tang*, drenching Savadkin, who had to cling to the bridge cowling to keep his balance as the *Tang* began to plunge down the mounting waves.

As the storm intensified, O'Kane ordered Savadkin to leave the bridge. The hatch from the bridge to the conning tower was sealed behind him. Soon, all aboard the *Tang* could hear the full might of the storm, a class-four typhoon. "The sound of mounting seas now came through the ballast tanks, great muffled roars, but they were mild compared to the screaming winds and crashing seas I could hear over the Voycall," recalled O'Kane.[24]

Suddenly, the *Tang* rolled so severely that O'Kane was thrown out of his bunk. He knew that he would have to issue orders from the control room to stand the best chance of weathering the storm without significant damage. Doc Larson gave O'Kane another injection to kill the pain in his foot, which Howard Walker then carefully slipped into a size-fourteen boot. Larson and Frank Springer helped their captain toward the control room.

O'Kane stepped over a sill into the control room. At that moment the *Tang* rolled violently to starboard, knocking O'Kane off his feet. "I landed on the after end of the high-pressure air manifold with my face about a foot from the bubble inclinometer on the forward end of the low-pressure blows. It read seventy degrees, and there she hung, obviously broached by the seas," he recalled.[25]

"Jesus Christ," said O'Kane, "is she ever coming back?"

Frank Springer suddenly fell back onto a switchboard and was jolted by a 110-volt current. He leapt away from the board.

"Sometimes they don't, you know!" said Springer.

The *Tang* righted herself again, much to the relief of the crew.

Springer scrambled up the ladder to the conning tower. O'Kane followed him, pulling himself up by the arms. Tensions were running high. Chief Quartermaster Sidney Jones raised the periscope to its full height, some fifty-five feet above the sea.[26] Then O'Kane steadied himself and looked through the scope. To his shock, he saw a "single monstrous wave, so big it had normal waves on its crest, which were blowing out into spume as it rolled in. Reflexes made [him] duck momentarily just before it hit, and then green water, solid green sea, went over the top of everything, burying *Tang*'s scope and all."[27]

O'Kane stepped away and Jones quickly lowered the periscope so it wouldn't be ripped off by the storm.

The *Tang* was in the heart of the typhoon. Her bridge was swamped by the crashing waves. Her bow rose from the wind-ripped water as she crested yet another huge wave. Then, as she tipped over and slid down the other side of the wave, her propellers whined when they broke the surface. Men were clinging to anything they could find to stop themselves from being thrown around. Larry Savadkin wedged himself between a bulkhead and a bunk.[28] Others lay in their bunks, clutching the side railings. In all their years at sea, they had never experienced such giant waves.

One man could take comfort in having survived worse: the strapping, dark-haired Chief Boatswain's Mate Bill Leibold. Aboard his first ship in the navy, the *Pruitt*, Leibold had actually been on deck in weather so severe that the *Pruitt* began to break up before finding safety.[29]

Leibold would vividly recall enduring this, his second life-threatening typhoon, more than sixty years later: "We couldn't dive for safety reasons, and so we had to ride it out. We had to button everything up—close the conning tower hatch. All you could see was foam and green water through the scopes. It seemed it went on forever. When we rolled, we wondered whether we would come back up because the rolls were so extreme. We were all worried we might capsize."[30]

O'Kane could have ordered the *Tang* to dive hours ago but he had wanted to stay surfaced on the off chance of sighting the Japanese weather ship. Now there was no time to dive. To make matters worse, the *Tang* was probably being blown along at the speed of the storm, in winds of 150 miles per hour or more, toward rugged islands in the Ryukyu chain to the north. O'Kane knew he had to avoid them or be wrecked.[31] But to do so would mean risking everything by turning the *Tang* toward the seas. If a powerful wave hit as she went broadside, she could capsize.

"All ahead standard," said O'Kane.

Eyes fixed on the *Tang's* inclinometer, which would show the extent of any roll.

"Twenty-five degrees," called out Chief Motor Machinist Marvin De Lapp.

The roll was considerably less than previous ones.

The moment to make the turn had come.

"All ahead full," ordered O'Kane. "Right full rudder."

Another massive wave struck the *Tang*. She swung over, but just as she seemed about to capsize, she somehow righted herself.

"All ahead two-thirds," ordered O'Kane. "Ease the rudder to fifteen. Meet her. Steer two-one-zero."[32]

The *Tang* was headed the right way. After enduring a few more massive waves, she had completed the turn. In every compartment, the sense of relief was palpable. The worst was surely over now? The typhoon continued to rage outside, but soon the *Tang* was rolling from side to side less and less violently.

O'Kane asked for an injury report. It wasn't long before Doc

Larson reported back that all hands were unharmed. The challenge now was to keep the *Tang* headed into the seas. For five long hours, the *Tang's* steersmen worked without complaint as the *Tang* rode the waves.

Floyd Caverly took his turn at the hydraulic wheel in the conning tower, cranking it back and forth. "You sat there and you fought that rudder," he recalled. "The sub was turning first one way and then the other as it hit big waves and troughs. I tried to keep on course but it was impossible. I just had to keep her heading into the seas in a general direction as much as possible."[33]

Which way was the storm moving? A crew member tried to open a hatch to get a barometer reading to find out, but the hatch would not budge because of the intense atmospheric pressure outside. So the crew allowed high-pressure air to bleed slowly into the boat until the hatch could be opened. The barometer read 28.4—higher than before. The increase meant the *Tang* was moving away from the heart of the typhoon.[34]

Finally, the exhausted crew was able to get some rest. In the forward torpedo room, the mechanics could now lie in their bunks above the torpedoes without clinging to the railings, knuckles white. They included Torpedoman Pete Narowanksi. The fair-haired, twenty-year-old was blessed with good luck, it seemed, having already lived to tell the tale of the sinking of his first ship. On the afternoon of November 12, 1942, Narowanski had been aboard the USS *Hugh L. Scott*, a troop transport, when she was hit on the starboard side by a single torpedo launched by a particularly deadly U-boat. *U-130* was captained by the formidable Ernst Kals, who had sunk no fewer than seventeen ships on his previous four patrols, an impressive record to compare with the *Tang's* own.

The USS *Scott* had been at anchor at Fedelah Point in Morocco when one of the five torpedoes fired by Kals exploded, sending flames stabbing into the early evening sky.[35] The order was given to abandon ship as the *Scott* quickly foundered. Narowanski was one of 60 survivors, out of a crew of 119, who were pulled out of the frigid water by men in landing craft that had been unloaded on a nearby beach in recent days. A Knight's Cross recipient, Ernst Kals survived the *U-130*'s patrol, but the *U-130* was sunk, under the command of a new captain, along with fifty-three of her crew after being depth-charged west of the Azores by the USS *Champlin* on March 12, 1943. By then, Pete Narowanski was back in the States, training at the New London submarine school in Connecticut.

Narowanski had completed two patrols aboard the USS *Halibut* before joining the *Tang* on her third patrol, knowing that she would return to San Francisco, his favorite liberty, for an extensive refit. In Pearl Harbor, he had met one of the *Tang*'s crew members who was looking to get off the boat. "He was the third lookout onboard and didn't want to go out again," explained Narowanski. "So I arranged a swap with him."[36]

The son of Russian immigrants, Narowanski had grown up in Baltimore. A devout member of the Russian Orthodox Church, and an avid hunter before the war, he was among the fittest of the men aboard, one of the few who did not smoke. His quiet, laid-back manner belied a steely determination to overcome every setback, no matter how daunting. He had been pulled out of the water after the torpedoing of the *Scott*. Now he had weathered one of the worst storms ever recorded. Surely he would not have to endure too much more before the war was over?

4

The Greatest Patrol

Dick O'Kane and his men had survived all that the ocean could throw at them—their greatest ordeal in over six months of tense action. It was five o'clock in the evening on October 6 when O'Kane finally felt that conditions were calm enough to fire up the diesel engines, and the sound of their reassuring throb once again filled the boat.

Frank Springer plotted a revised course toward the *Tang*'s patrol area in the Formosa Strait; O'Kane ordered full power to make up for lost time and the distance the *Tang* had been forced off course by the typhoon—as much as sixty miles. Going by the observations made by the men on the bridge and Chief Quartermaster Sidney Jones's recordings, they had been in the eye of one of the fiercest typhoons in living memory, with waves estimated at ninety-five feet. At one point, so huge was the mass of water crashing down on her, the *Tang*'s bridge had been under water for fourteen seconds.

Two days later, on October 8, the *Tang* was well clear of the storm and making steady progress, operating at three-engine speed. Suddenly, lookouts spotted what looked like a plane in the far distance.

Ooga! Ooga!

The *Tang*'s Klaxons sounded the alarm.

Lookouts scrambled from their positions in the sheers and down the hatch, riding on one another's shoulders as their hands slid down the ladder sides. Within sixty seconds, the *Tang* was below the surface. The plane had in all likelihood been a bird on the horizon, but O'Kane was taking no risks in being discovered as he closed on the "hot area"—the Formosa Strait.[1]

There was now time for twenty-one-year-old Floyd Caverly to check on his secret distillery. He had set it up in a small space near the bilges. By the time the *Tang* reached San Francisco for her refit following this patrol, he figured he would have a gallon or more of homemade hooch—plenty for a well-deserved shore party.

Bill "Boats" Leibold was well aware of the still but kept its existence secret from O'Kane. He too liked a tipple every now and again, but only when on shore. "We all knew that if the Old Man found out about it," Leibold said, "we would get our asses kicked out of submarines."[2] According to others on the *Tang*, Caverly was a master at securing fruit, even grape juice, to distill. "We made a little 'torpedo juice'—that's what we called it," recalled Caverly. "It was run off and distilled and then the pharmacist's mate, Larson, would check it for purity. We made some good stuff."[3]

Caverly was on good terms with Bill Leibold, but others on the boat trod warily around the chief boatswain's mate, who was as driven as his captain and demanded the highest standards. Not for nothing was Leibold referred to by some of the men as "that S.O.B." "It always made me feel good that the guys called me Sweet Old Bill," Leibold would later joke.[4]

The single-minded Californian with an intense stare took his cue from O'Kane when dealing with the enlisted men under his charge. "I thought Leibold was related to Hitler the way he cracked the whip on that boat," recalled Clay Decker, the broad-faced ex-miner from Colorado.

Decker was intensely proud that he had become fully qualified as a submariner, earning a pair of silver dolphins on the right sleeve of his shore whites after just his first patrol. He had reason to be pleased with himself—earning the dolphins as a torpedo-man, under Leibold's supervision, had been hard work. "I broke down after the first patrol and went from the torpedo room to the black gang [the motor mechanics] because he [Leibold] did not have any authority in the engine room," explained Decker.[5]

THERE THEY WERE, far off in the distance—the towering thirteen thousand-foot mountains of Formosa. They had arrived in the hot area. It was noon on October 10 when one of the *Tang*'s lookouts made the landfall through his powerful binoculars. With the jagged peak of Yonakuni Shima rising to the *Tang*'s starboard, O'Kane ordered an increase in speed. The *Tang* went to four engines to get into the Formosa Strait before nightfall.

The following morning, at about 4, the *Tang* made her first contact. O'Kane was lying in his bunk, looking at the luminous numbers on his cabin clock, when one of the crew, sent by the duty chief, entered his cabin.

"We've got a ship, Captain," he whispered.

It was less than two hours after the *Tang* had reached its patrol area and already it had closed on its first target. This fifth patrol promised rich pickings indeed.

A pulse of excitement passed through the boat.[6] Veteran submariner Ned Beach would later describe how it felt to begin a chase as engines roared hypnotically and waves slapped against the hull: "The vibration communicated to the soles of your feet sets your pulses jumping and your heart beating faster, and it all adds up to the anthem of the chase, which drums in your mind, growing ever louder and more powerful, beating in an ever-rising tympanic crescendo which drugs your senses and drives you beyond normal capabilities, which takes possession of you, wipes out all external considerations, and makes itself the undisputed master of your soul."[7]

O'Kane hobbled from his cabin to the red-lit control room.

"Range seventeen thousand, closing," said a torpedoman's mate named John Foster from Detroit.

The general alarm, referred to as "The Bells of St. Mary's," sounded throughout the submarine.

O'Kane patiently waited until just after dawn. Then a lookout got a clear view of the target, a modern diesel freighter, loaded down and therefore providing a low silhouette on the skyline.

Bill Leibold helped O'Kane, who now walked by putting his weight onto the heel of his broken foot, up to the bridge. Together they tracked the enemy with their binoculars.

The *Tang* was soon in the perfect position to make a submerged attack.

"Clear the bridge!"

Klaxons sounded.

Ooga! Ooga!

The bridge cleared fast, men dropping below, lookouts leaving the bridge last.

The words "battle stations" passed quietly from compartment to compartment, and men went to their assigned positions.

In the control room, where the main systems for diving and surfacing were housed, Larry Savadkin trimmed the boat as she dived to forty-five feet, opening vents that allowed air to escape and tons of saltwater to rush in through flood ports. A few feet from where Savadkin stood was a "Christmas tree"—a panel of lights that showed the status of every opening in the hull. All were green, indicating that the *Tang* was watertight.

Savadkin leveled the *Tang* so that the SJ (surface-search) radar's antenna was still above the water.

Adjacent to the control room was the cramped radio room, often thick with the smell of food from the nearby galley. Floyd Caverly sat in it now with his earphones on, listening to the sound of the enemy boat's screws, timing it to the metronome. For a few seconds, he switched the noise to a speaker so the crew could hear it.

Thump. Thump. Thump.

Thank God it was not a destroyer, whose screws made a heart-stopping *swish, swish, swish*.

Idle conversation had long since stopped. Faces were etched with tension in the control room, where O'Kane's tracking team plotted the enemy's course on a chart table lit from above by a single, metal-shaded bulb.

O'Kane directed the *Tang* toward her first target. Frank Springer, standing near him, issued crisp orders to the firing party as the *Tang* closed on the enemy ship. In the maneuvering room, Chief Electrician's Mate James Culp stood tensely, a little stooped because of painful arthritis, awaiting orders from the control room. He and his electrician's mates, some wearing protective gloves, now had the key task of directing the *Tang*'s electrical current. Culp looked carefully at the amperage, knowing that if O'Kane ordered "full ahead" it would put a dramatic drain on the batteries.

Through his sea-splashed periscope, O'Kane could now see his target heading for the shore.

"Make ready tubes one, two, and three forward," said O'Kane. "And if there's a wide zig, tubes seven, eight, and nine aft."

In the forward torpedo room, Pete Narowanski and muscle-bound Hayes Trukke, as well as the other torpedo mechanics, knew their six "fish" would be the first of the patrol to be fired. They let compressed air—six hundred pounds per square inch—into the tanks to use in firing each torpedo, and flooded one, two, and three tubes.

"Open the outer doors."

The doors were opened.

Narowanksi stood beside the torpedo that was his responsibility, his hand over a firing pin he could use if the automatic firing system in the conning tower didn't work.

O'Kane still stood at the periscope, his face pressed to its eyepiece in utter concentration. In the dawn twilight, he could make out a decent-sized cargo ship.

The *Tang* began her approach. Finally, the target was just where O'Kane wanted it. He placed his periscope's hairline sight just aft of its stacks.

"Stand by for constant bearings," said O'Kane. "Up scope!"

"Constant bearing—mark!"

"Set," said fresh-faced Lieutenant Mel Enos as he pressed a button.

Enos was standing nearby, operating the torpedo data computer, which automatically computed and set the correct angle of fire on the torpedoes' controlling gyroscopes. In pressing the button, he had locked in the enemy's last bearing.[8]

"Fire!" O'Kane ordered.

Frank Springer's palm hit the firing plunger.

There was a jolting *whoosh* followed by another and a shudder as compressed air forced two torpedoes out of their tubes.

The sonar officer tracked the course of the torpedoes.

All hot, straight, and normal.

The quartermaster counted the seconds as the Mark 18 electric torpedoes sped toward the target at twenty-six knots. The run was set for forty-seven seconds.

". . . 45, 44, 43 . . . "

The entire crew, it seemed, waited with bated breath.

". . . 19, 18, 17 . . . "

Caverly turned on a speaker and switched between the sound of the enemy's screws and the high-pitched whine of the torpedoes.

Whoom! Whoom! Two direct hits. The cargo ship, the 1,658-ton *Josho Maru*, exploded and quickly slipped below the waves, stern first. O'Kane looked through the periscope. A breeze blew a cloud of smoke clear of the *Josho Maru*. All he could see was the ship's bow, slipping into the ocean in the dawn light.

Ooga! Ooga! Ooga!

Klaxons sounded. The mottled camouflage grey of the *Tang* broke the surface, her shears and then bridge and finally guns emerging from the roiling waters. A hatch lifted as water drained from the bridge, and O'Kane and others emerged carrying binoculars. There were plenty of pieces of flotsam and jetsam, even some swamped landing craft, but no survivors.

Fortunately for the *Tang*, her cover had not been blown. The Japanese attributed the *Josho Maru*'s sudden loss to being hit by a mine. They had no idea that an American submarine had entered the Formosa Strait. For a while longer, the *Tang* could maneuver with relative impunity. And that was what O'Kane did, ordering the *Tang* to cruise on the surface toward heavily trafficked waters to the southwest.

It was some five hours later, around 10 a.m. on October 11, when a strong northerly wind rose and the ocean began to be whipped up. At midday, a lookout spotted the masts of another northbound freighter. "Though we could reach his track by moving in at high speed and have some battery left for evasion," recalled O'Kane, "tracking till dark seemed more prudent under the circumstances."[9]

The *Tang* pursued the freighter for twenty-seven miles. The seas were heavy, and the target bucked up and down as the *Tang* ran undetected at seven knots, eighty feet below.[10] As it grew dark, the *Tang* surfaced four thousand yards astern of the enemy ship. The twilight faded to pitch darkness. Spume rolled off the waters.

"Head for him, Hank," said O'Kane to twenty-eight-year-old Lieutenant Flanagan, a bony-faced, dour man who had been in the navy since the mid-1930s. Flanagan was one of several hands who could find his way around a submarine blindfolded, and he rather abrasively let every enlisted man know it.[11]

Howard Walker brought O'Kane a cup of coffee. "We going to get this one, too, Captain?" he asked.

O'Kane nodded.

Later that evening, about nine o'clock, the *Tang* was in position, just 450 yards from the target.

"Fire!" O'Kane commanded.

A single torpedo sped through the dark waters, aimed to inflict maximum damage and injury by hitting the target's engine room. Seconds later, the 711-ton *Oita Maru*'s boilers exploded, sending a "pillar of fire and illuminated steam skyward," lighting up the coastline. Men rushed from the *Tang*'s conning tower to the bridge to see what had happened. Only the first to get there were in time to see the *Oita Maru* slip with a last, pathetic hiss beneath the waves.

Then there was gunfire—the steady *ack-ack* of antiaircraft batteries. But no salvos landed nearby. It was quickly clear that the 40mm guns on the shore were not aiming at the *Tang* but into the sky, at phantom planes. Incredibly, the Japanese still had not realized that the *Tang* was in their midst. O'Kane was happy to let the Japanese think that American planes from China were responsible for the attack on the *Oita Maru*.

The *Tang* then moved down the coast. Late that night, Japanese patrol boats were finally detected. The enemy was no doubt beginning to react to the swift sinking of two ships in a matter of hours. O'Kane ordered the *Tang* to deeper water as a precaution. Once there, he gave orders for his crew to take a break. They had endured the typhoon and then two attacks without a letup. Everyone needed a good rest, not least O'Kane, who was beginning to feel the accumulated fatigue of more than ten war patrols.

But there was precious little respite: Later that night, the radar detected a large target. O'Kane was soon on the bridge, peering through binoculars. He saw tell-tale green and red side lights. Then a white hull emblazoned with a red cross. It was a hospital ship. Someone on the bridge suggested they sink it.

"We play by the rules," said O'Kane.[12]

"The bastard's probably transporting 10,000 troops, all with athlete's foot," said Bill Ballinger.[13]

But O'Kane was having none of it. There was a line that he

would not cross no matter how much he wanted to "kill more Japs."[14]

DICK O'KANE FULLY UNDERSTOOD Ballinger's urge to destroy the hospital ship. O'Kane's contempt for the enemy was absolute; not once, for example, had he capitalized the words "Jap" and "Nip" as other captains did in their patrol reports—the Japanese were more often than not referred to as "debris." But sinking a clearly marked hospital ship was not something he wanted on his conscience.

O'Kane had already witnessed the slaughter of helpless men. Indeed, during the *Wahoo's* third patrol, he had seen more than enough "unrestricted submarine warfare." According to a junior officer on board the *Wahoo* named George Grider, back then O'Kane had been a very different man than the one who now commanded the *Tang*. As Mush Morton's executive officer, he had "talked a great deal—reckless, aggressive talk. . . . During the second patrol Dick had grown harder to live with, friendly one minute and pulling his rank on his junior officers the next. One day he would be a martinet, and the next he would display an over-lenient, what-the-hell attitude that was far from reassuring. With Mush and Dick in the saddle, how would the *Wahoo* fare?"[15]

It was a good question, and in that January of 1943, the crew of the *Wahoo* did not have to wait long for an answer.

The *Wahoo* had been ordered to reconnoiter Wewak, a Japanese base in New Guinea. Without the aid of a chart, the *Wahoo* approached the port, Morton handing periscope duties to O'Kane. As George Grider later wrote: "This left the skipper in a better position to interpret all factors involved, do a better conning job, and make decisions more dispassionately. There is no doubt it is an excellent theory, and it worked beautifully for him, but few captains other than Mush ever had such serene faith in a subordinate that they could resist grabbing the scope in moments of crisis."[16]

Morton's orders had stated clearly that he was to reconnoiter, but Morton declared, to his crew's astonishment, that he would do far more—he would enter the harbor and sink any ships there. As far as Grider was concerned, Morton had gone from "mere rashness to outright foolhardiness."[17]

The *Wahoo* headed into Wewak, evading several patrol craft with Morton joking throughout, even as he narrowly avoided running aground.

Inside the port, O'Kane spotted a destroyer, and then suddenly seemed transformed. "I found myself marveling," recalled Grider, "at the change that had come over Dick O'Kane. It was as if, during all the talkative, boastful months before, he had been lost, seeking his true element, and now it was found. He was calm, terse, and utterly cool. My opinion of him underwent a permanent change. It was not the first time I had observed that the conduct of men under fire cannot be predicted accurately from their everyday actions, but it was the most dramatic example I was ever to see of a man transformed under pressure from what seemed almost adolescent petulance to a prime fighting machine."[18]

As Morton readied to fire, the destroyer began to get under way. Morton quickly fired three torpedoes. None hit. The Japanese destroyer, with more than a hundred men on her decks, headed for the *Wahoo*. Morton did not flinch, ordering the periscope to be kept up, and then prepared for a "down the throat shot." At twelve hundred yards, Morton again fired a torpedo and missed. One of the *Wahoo*'s terrified crew recalled having "an uncontrollable urge to urinate."[19] At eight hundred yards, Morton then fired a sixth torpedo. This time he didn't miss. The destroyer erupted with a huge explosion.

The next day, the *Wahoo* came across a small convoy. Morton fired on three ships, hitting all of them, before going deep to avoid being rammed. It wasn't long before Morton surfaced and looked around. He had sunk one ship. Another was badly damaged. The third, a large transport, was motionless.

Wanting to finish off the transport, Morton approached her and fired but the torpedo did not detonate—no doubt stirring bitter memories of many other torpedoes that had failed to detonate during the *Wahoo*'s early patrols in 1942.[20] Morton's second torpedo, however, was no dud—it blew the transport "higher than a kite" in Morton's words. Some of the 1,126 men aboard, including 491 Indian POWs, began to jump over the side into the water "like ants off a hot plate."[21]

Morton ordered his crew to man the deck guns. The *Wahoo* was now in a "sea of Japanese." "The water was so thick with enemy soldiers," recalled George Grider, "that it was literally impossible to cruise through them without pushing them aside like driftwood. These were troops we knew had been bound for New Guinea, to fight and kill our own men, and Mush, whose overwhelming biological hatred of the enemy we were only now beginning to sense, looked about him with exultation at the carnage."[22]

"There must be close to 10,000 of them in the water," said one of Morton's officers.

"I figure about 9,500 of the sons of bitches," replied Morton.[23]

"What do you think?" O'Kane asked Morton. "They look like marines to me."[24]

"You're damn right they are," replied Morton. "They're part of

Hirohito's crack Imperial Marine outfit. I ran into some of them before the war in Shanghai."[25]

"If those troops get rescued," O'Kane said, "we're going to lose a lot of American boys' lives digging them out of foxholes and shooting them out of palm trees."

"I know," Morton replied, "and it's a damn stinking shame . . . when we've got them cold turkey in the water. . . . But there's still [an] oil tanker and cargo out there. We're going after those babies as soon as we get a battery charge."[26]

Morton then ordered his crew to destroy several lifeboats. According to Morton, some of the survivors fired back with pistols— that was all Morton needed to order his men to treat the Japanese as "fair game." What ensued was the worst slaughter inflicted by an American submarine's gun crews in World War II, lasting for "nightmarish minutes" in George Grider's words.[27]

In his patrol report, Morton wrote: "After about an hour of this, we destroyed all the boats and most of the troops." Back in Hawaii, the *Wahoo* was welcomed home with a *Honolulu Advertiser* headline: WAHOO RUNNING JAPS A'GUNNING. Morton and the *Wahoo* had become famous overnight. In the official endorsements of Morton's patrol report, no mention was made of what some submariners considered the cold-blooded killing of defenseless troops.[28]

As it turned out, Morton never had to justify his actions after the war. By then, he and the *Wahoo*'s crew were dead, entombed by iron somewhere in the Sea of Japan after Japanese patrol planes had caught her, fatally exposed, on the surface. O'Kane would have gone to the bottom along with his mentor had he not been given his own command of the *Tang* before *Wahoo* set out on her final patrol in July 1943.

Fellow submarine captain Ned Beach knew both Morton and

O'Kane. "O'Kane was not an over-sentimental man," he recalled. "Only one who has experienced the extinction of a whole unit of comrades without trace can fully appreciate the icy fingers which must have clutched around his heart when he received the grim news."[29]

Ever since, Beach added, Dick O'Kane had been on a "mission of vengeance."

5

Battle Royal

D ICK O'KANE LAY IN HIS BUNK, listening to the intercom.

Suddenly, the duty chief's messenger burst into his cabin.

"We've got another convoy, captain!" said the excited messenger. "The chief says it's the best one since the Yellow Sea."[1]

It was well after dark on October 22, 1944, when O'Kane began to track convoy U-03, which was comprised of six ships, two of them well-armed destroyers, the *Tsuga* and *Hasu*. O'Kane considered his options. He would rather not have to penetrate the escort screen on the surface at night, but if he waited, the convoy would reach shallower water.

Howard Walker handed O'Kane a fresh cup of coffee, and O'Kane began his approach. It was around midnight when one of the Japanese escorts left the convoy to make a search. O'Kane seized his moment, ordering two-thirds speed. By 1:30 a.m. the *Tang* was poised to strike. In the conning tower, Executive Officer Frank Springer reported that all forward torpedo tubes were open. O'Kane peered through the periscope. He had a large tanker right where he wanted it.

O'Kane climbed the ladder from the conning tower to the bridge, where he soon stood beside Bill Leibold, whom he regarded as his "extra pair of eyes."

"Constant bearing—mark!" ordered O'Kane.

"Set," replied Mel Enos.

"Fire!"

There was the familiar shudder as one of the *Tang*'s fish headed toward its target. It did not miss. More torpedoes soon followed. Explosions lit the sky as shock waves rocked the *Tang*.

"They all hit as we aimed 'em, captain," said Chief Quartermaster Sidney Jones.[2]

O'Kane was not finished. There were still more ships to sink. He quickly prepared a stern shot on another target.

Leibold grabbed O'Kane, almost dislocating his shoulder.[3]

"She's coming in to ram!" shouted Leibold.[4]

Leibold pointed to a Japanese ship that was bearing down on the *Tang*.[5] O'Kane had not seen it, so focused had he been on the target to the stern. There was no time to dive or fire torpedoes.

"All ahead emergency! Right full rudder!" ordered O'Kane.[6]

The engines roared. Clouds of diesel smoke belched from her exhausts. The *Tang* moved to port, cutting across the bow of the approaching ship, the 1,920-ton *Wakatake Maru*. Japanese sailors on the main deck grabbed rifles and pistols and began to open fire, aiming at the *Tang*'s bridge party. It was a close-run thing, with the *Tang* avoiding the *Wakatake Maru* with only yards to spare.

"Clear the bridge!" ordered O'Kane.

Ooga! Ooga!

Men scrambled down the hatch. Then, just as O'Kane prepared to follow them, he saw an out-of-control freighter. It was headed toward the *Wakatake Maru*.

"Hold her up!" shouted O'Kane. "Hold her up!"

The *Tang's* decks were partly under water. In seconds, she was again fully surfaced.

"New set up!"

"Give me a range and mark," said Mel Enos.

"You don't need one," replied O'Kane. "Just fire! You can't put a torpedo out without hitting this bastard."[7]

Torpedoes emerged from the stern torpedo tubes, aimed at the *Wakatake Maru*. They hit just as the out-of-control freighter collided with the *Wakatake Maru* "with a rending, groaning crash of tortured and distorted steel."[8] Both ships disappeared for a few seconds in a giant ball of fire, smoke, and showering debris.

It was 1:40 in the morning. On the bridge, O'Kane surveyed the devastation. Two torpedoes had hit *Wakatake Maru*. One had been beautifully targeted at the rear part of the engine room on the port side to inflict maximum damage. It had clearly done so.

Suddenly, the sky was also lit with the muzzle flashes of Japanese deck guns. O'Kane watched in delight as the convoy's escorts began to fire at each other in panicked confusion.

Wakatake Maru quickly broke in two and, forty seconds later, dropped below the waves. In less than a minute, the *Tang* had dispatched 128 men belonging to a salvage unit, 30 crewmen, 11 ship's gunners, and 7 passengers.[9]

The *Tang* then slipped away into the night. Understandably, her crew buzzed with excitement. They had pulled off a truly spectacular attack, arguably the most devastating of the war. The *Tang* had hit and then sunk all of the convoy's cargo-carrying ships. She had also caused severe damage to an escort ship in the convoy, which then burned before beaching on the Pescadores. In all, the battle had lasted less than ten minutes.[10] Once again, Commander Dick O'Kane had proven, in Floyd Caverly's words, to be "quite the marksman."[11]

IT WAS LATE ON OCTOBER 24, 1944, when blips again appeared on the Tang's surface radar screen. O'Kane ordered the Tang to close on what appeared to be another convoy. Soon, the radar screen showed many more blips, targets galore. The Tang began her approach, possibly her last given that only a half dozen or so torpedoes were left.

O'Kane turned to Frank Springer: "Do you think we'll have time before daylight to fire from the surface?"

"Yes," replied Springer. "By the time we get into position it's going to be just about two o'clock or two ten. We'll have to fire then or we won't be able to make it. We'll be exposed to the surface."[12]

The Tang maneuvered into position.

"Fire!" ordered O'Kane.

Mark 18 electric torpedoes shot from the Tang, aimed to hit beneath the masts of two freighters and under the main stack of a tanker. O'Kane was at the top of his game. Explosions soon followed, their shock waves spreading across the sea and rocking the Tang slightly.

The Tang continued on the surface. More enemy ships were soon within striking distance. O'Kane ordered his men to set up for stern shots at a tanker and a transport. Torpedoes were fired at both. Before long, there was an ear-splitting explosion; the tanker erupted into a massive fireball. Clearly, she had been loaded to the brim with fuel.[13]

The tanker blazed so brightly that the *Tang* suddenly seemed to have emerged into daylight. O'Kane and his bridge party looked around. At least one torpedo had hit the transport, which was still afloat, dead in the water. Suddenly, Japanese escorts began to concentrate their fire on the *Tang*. Volleys of machine gun bullets splattered in the sea. It was time to disappear.

Below the bridge, in the conning tower, Frank Springer pleaded with Chief Electrician James Culp for more power.[14]

Culp said he was worried that any further increase in power might overload the generators. The noise from the engines was already almost deafening, their pistons hammering away as enginemen, wearing earplugs, made hand signals and a red warning light blinked steadily.

"To hell with the overload," Frank Springer ordered. "Pour on the coal."

Culp instructed his men to do so. The pistons began to pump more furiously as the *Tang*'s four Fairbanks Morse diesel engines thundered, powering the *Tang*'s generators, pushing five million watts through the submarine's four main motors. The *Tang* was soon moving away at full speed, around twenty-three knots, partially hidden by a cloud of exhaust fumes.

Other captains might now have plotted a new course and not looked back. Not Dick O'Kane. At ten thousand yards from the convoy, he slowed the *Tang*. He was going back for more—to finish off the transport he'd seen dead in the water.

O'Kane ordered his torpedo mechanics to pull the last two torpedoes from their tubes and examine them. With so few left, he wanted to make sure there would be no mistakes. Pete Narowanski, Hayes Trukke, and the other torpedo mechanics carefully checked the *Tang's* last two fish. They then loaded them into forward tubes numbered five and six.

Thirty minutes later, the *Tang* was ready to deliver the coup de grâce to the stricken transport. All twenty-two torpedoes that had been fired so far had worked perfectly. "This promised to be a typical *Tang* patrol," Vice Admiral Lockwood would later write. "Three or four weeks packed with thrills and action and then, 'Course 090' [the compass course back to Pearl] with empty torpedo tubes and a full bag."[15]

The *Tang* moved forward at six knots, her bow pointing at the transport. No escorts were in sight.

Floyd Caverly looked at the screen of his SJ radar in the conning tower.

"Range: fifteen hundred yards," said Caverly.[16]

The submarine crept slowly closer.

Nine hundred yards from the target, O'Kane was ready with his remaining two torpedoes—for all he knew, they were the last he might fire in combat during the war.

"Stand by below," O'Kane ordered.

"Ready below, captain," replied Springer.

"Fire!"

A small jolt was felt throughout the boat as the next-to-last torpedo was fired.

On the bridge, Bill Leibold stood beside O'Kane, peering through his binoculars. He saw the electric torpedo's phosphorescent wake as it headed straight toward the crippled transport nine hundred yards ahead of it. It was running "hot, straight, and normal."[17]

Now just one torpedo was left. Once it had been fired, the *Tang* could head back to safety, having completed one of the most destructive patrols of the war.

O'Kane called for a time check. It was 2:30 a.m. on October 25, 1944.

"Set!"

In the conning tower, Larry Savadkin operated the torpedo data computer. He pressed a button that set the final firing angle of the *Tang*'s last torpedo.

"Fire!" ordered O'Kane.

Frank Springer stood a few feet from Savadkin in the conning tower. He pressed the firing plunger. Again, a jolting *whoosh* as the last torpedo, Number 24, left the *Tang*. The submarine shuddered as compressed air forced the torpedo from its tube and seawater flooded back into the tube.

In the forward torpedo room, Pete Narowanski slammed his fist into the palm of his left hand.

"Hot dog, course zero nine zero," he cried. "Heading for the Golden Gate!"[18]

"Let's head for the barn," someone else shouted.

There was a massive explosion as Number 23 torpedo hit its target, sending flames and debris shooting into the sky and quickly sinking the 6,957-ton *Ebaru Maru*, officially the twenty-fourth victim during O'Kane's eighteen months in command of the *Tang*.

On the bridge, Bill Leibold scanned the waters with his binoculars. He stood next to O'Kane. Suddenly, he saw the last torpedo, Number 24, broach and then begin to porpoise, phosphorescence trailing it. A few seconds later, it made a sharp turn to port and then, unbelievably, began to come about.[19]

"There goes that one! Erratic!" shouted O'Kane.

The last torpedo was now heading like a boomerang, back to

its firing point . . . back toward the *Tang*. Something had gone terribly wrong. Perhaps its rudder had jammed or the gyroscope in its steering engine had malfunctioned.

"Emergency speed!" cried O'Kane.

Below, twenty-year-old Motor Machinist's Mate Jesse DaSilva had just left his post in the engine room, having decided to get a cup of coffee. The Los Angeles native was standing with one foot in the mess.[20] Over the intercom, he could hear the bridge crew react as the torpedo headed back toward the *Tang*.

"Captain, that's a circular run!" he heard Leibold say.

"All ahead emergency!" shouted O'Kane. "Right full rudder!"[21]

"Bend them on," added O'Kane. "Control, just bend them on."

In the engine room, Chief Electrician's Mate James Culp did his best to comply, knowing the *Tang* needed all the power she could get if there was to be a chance of saving lives.[22]

The torpedo was now making straight for the three hundred-foot submarine. The men on the bridge stood, transfixed, their eyes "popping out of their sockets."[23] The *Tang* was moving at about six knots, twenty less than her final torpedo.

"Left full rudder!" ordered O'Kane.

Bill Leibold watched in stricken silence as the torpedo headed right at them, coming dead-on toward the *Tang*. Then he lost sight of it as it continued down the port side.[24]

Maybe it will miss. Maybe it will veer away and begin another erratic circle. Maybe the Tang *will evade just in time.*

In a second or so, Leibold would find out.[25]

PART TWO

Escape from the Deep

Neither timid nor reckless men should go to sea.

— Arleigh A. Burke, Admiral, U.S. Navy

6

The Deep

I N T H E C O N N I N G T O W E R, Floyd Caverly waited like the
other men for the inevitable.

*Surely there's enough time to get out of the way—to get the hell
out of here? Surely?*

*Speed. Speed is all we need . . . just enough to get out of the way.
If only the* Tang *would just set by the stern and set off like a speedboat.*[1]

But the *Tang* was not a speedboat. She could not avoid the
charging torpedo. It hit the *Tang*'s stern with a massive explosion
somewhere between the maneuvering room and the after torpedo
room, killing as many as half the crew instantly and flooding all
aft compartments as far forward as the crew's quarters, midway
along the boat.[2]

Caverly was standing looking at a radarscope when it happened. He knew the outer hull was almost a full inch of nickel-alloyed steel, perhaps the best of its kind in the world. The *Tang* was rugged, but the sheer violence of the impact was astounding. The Mark 18 electric torpedo was packed with a powerful new explosive developed in the early days of the war to give submarines the extra punch required to sink thick-skinned enemy boats.

Caverly thought that the *Tang* had been snapped in two. The waves of concussion from the explosion made him feel as if he were experiencing a massive earthquake. He did not know which way to step to catch his balance. The deck plates rattled and shook. Lightbulbs went out.

In the conning tower, there was chaos.

"We've been hit!"[3] cried Executive Officer Frank Springer.

IN THE FORWARD TORPEDO ROOM, Pete Narowanski found himself flat on his back from the huge explosion.[4] He picked himself up. *What happened?* There had been no alarm. One moment he had been rejoicing, looking forward to carousing in San Francisco. Now he could feel the *Tang* sinking. Had the *Tang* been hit by a Japanese shell? Loose equipment began to slide through the compartment.[5] Then he felt a bump as the stern hit the bottom. A few seconds later, he heard air rushing through the main ballast tank blowers—someone in the control room was trying to blow the *Tang* back to the surface. But it didn't work. Clearly, much of the after section of the submarine was flooded.

Narowanski looked around at his comrades in the forward torpedo room. Among the men now holding on to anything within reach and nursing serious bruises were blonde-haired Hayes

Trukke; the burly Leland Weekley, chief torpedoman; and Virginian John Fluker.

Narowanski was in good company. After four patrols and several hair-raising episodes in their presence, he could rely on these
men totally. They wouldn't "flip out" in a crisis.[6]

Narowanski's fellow torpedomen also knew they could depend
on him one hundred percent. "Ski," as he was nicknamed, and the
other men in the forward torpedo room remained calm. They were
well trained and had many years' experience between them. As
they tried to figure out what exactly had happened to the *Tang*,
they scanned the compartment for damage. There was surprisingly little. Then their training kicked in. They closed the watertight door leading to the next compartment. One of the men, who
was still wearing headphones, tried to contact other compartments but without success. Someone else turned on the emergency lights.[7]

Narowanski and the men in the forward torpedo room were
lucky. Unlike men trapped in other compartments, the torpedomen knew they had a way out from theirs—they were a few feet
from one of only two escape trunks on the *Tang*. The other was in
the after torpedo room, which was flooded, its occupants either
killed instantly by the explosion or now drowned. But Narowanski and the men with him could not use the escape trunk yet. They
would have to wait until everyone left alive made it to the forward
torpedo room. Only then could they try to get out. For the time
being, all they could do was hold on and pray.[8]

ON THE BRIDGE, Bill Leibold saw a cloud of what looked like
black smoke. In fact it was water thrown up from the explosion.

He and other men on the bridge felt the boat being wrenched, as if it were being split in half.[9]

A few feet from Leibold, Dick O'Kane watched, aghast, as the tops of the after ballast tanks blew into the air. Water washed across the wooden main decking, around the five-inch main gun, and then toward the aft cigarette deck where the *Tang*'s 40mm gun was positioned, several feet from where O'Kane now stood on the bridge.

"Do we have propulsion?" asked O'Kane, speaking into his bridge phone.

There was no answer.

O'Kane again shouted into the bridge phone.

The men in the conning tower below could hear him. But O'Kane received no reply. The explosion had knocked out the microphone on his bridge phone.[10]

"Radar!" shouted O'Kane, "I want to know how far it is to the closest destroyer and what the course is on that destroyer."[11]

Caverly picked up his microphone in the conning tower.

"The radar is out of commission," said Caverly. "I have no bearing or range right now."

"Radar," barked O'Kane, "I'm asking for information and I want it *now!*"

Caverly realized that O'Kane's microphone was out of action so he stepped over to the hatch and called up: "The radar is out of commission."

Caverly then gave the *Tang*'s last bearing and range, but O'Kane did not hear him. He had stepped away from the hatch.

"I want information, radar!"[12] O'Kane shouted again.

Frank Springer grabbed Caverly by the nape of the neck and seat of his pants and began to shove him up the hatch.

"Get up there and talk to the skipper!" said Springer.[13]

Caverly climbed up the ladder to the bridge. As he stepped onto the bridge's deck, he saw a lookout man, Radioman Charles Andriolo, who had grown up in Massachusetts. He was clinging to a guardrail, his binoculars hanging from his neck.

Andriolo looked terrified. He said he couldn't swim.

Caverly stepped over toward O'Kane, who was a few feet from Bill Leibold.

A second or so later, Leibold noticed Caverly standing right next to him. Both men looked aft, in the direction of the explosion.

"I'm not going back down below," said Caverly.[14]

Water started to rise up toward the bridge. It had soon covered the aft third of the submarine.

"Close the hatch!" cried O'Kane.

But it was too late. The *Tang* began to sink, tons of water pouring into the conning tower. The after section of the submarine had flooded.[15]

Leibold glanced around and saw Andriolo frozen to the spot, in "a death grip," clinging to a guardrail, as more of the *Tang* slipped below. Andriolo was one of the *Tang*'s four lookouts who would never be seen again. It is thought that they became entangled in the sheers as the *Tang* sank and were quickly drowned.

Caverly knew it was now time for every man to look after himself.

To hell with those Japanese destroyers or anything else.

Caverly moved to the edge of the *Tang*'s wooden decking. Suddenly, she seemed to roll to port a little and then came back up and righted herself. The water flooding her deck appeared to subside.

Maybe everything is going to be all right.

But then Caverly saw the stern begin to slip beneath the waves. He stepped over to the guardrail. As soon as the water came up to his hips, he swam off, striking out, determined not to get sucked down after the *Tang*.[16]

Caverly paddled away from the boat. When he looked over his shoulder, he could see the *Tang* disappear gradually, as if on a practice dive, slipping gently beneath the ocean, stern first. Then he saw that she had stopped sinking. Perhaps five or six feet of her bow remained exposed.

Thankfully, the *Tang* had sunk in relatively shallow water—it was no more than 180 feet to the seabed. Because she was 315 feet long, her stern had hit bottom after a few seconds. Clearly, enough air was still inside to keep her bow above the surface, like some upturned bottle.

It was fortunate that the *Tang* had not gone down in the north Atlantic or near the Aleutians, where Caverly could expect to last only a few minutes in icy water. He was now trying to stay afloat in the relatively warm and calm Pacific off the coast of China, but the slightly choppy sea felt cold all the same.

Caverly swam farther away from the stricken Tang. *Was anybody still alive in the submarine?* There was no way for him to know whether any men in the boat had been able to seal the *Tang* for "watertight integrity." The stars shone in the sky. There were no clouds. It was around two o'clock in the morning. He knew that for sure. He had looked at his wristwatch just before the last torpedoes had been fired, when O'Kane had called for a time check.

I wonder which side of the international date line we're on, he thought. *If I'm on one side, then it's now October 25th, my wedding anniversary. So, I've been sunk on my wedding anniversary!*[17]

Caverly thought about his loved ones as he tried to keep his head above water. "There was nothing to do but think," he later recalled. "It's hard to explain what goes through your head in a situation like that. I thought about my childhood, my folks, Leone, my wife, and my daughter, Mary Anne. I thought of all [the] things I had planned to do that I wasn't now going to get to do."[18]

Caverly's childhood had been tough. His mother died eighteen months after he was born in northern Minnesota, the son of a blacksmith from Michigan who first came to the area to work with logging crews. He met blonde-haired Leone, who was a year older than him, when he worked on a threshing gang on a farm near her family's home before the war. They had fallen in love after painting a house together. Within eight months, they were married at her home, and, in 1942, Leone gave birth to Mary Anne, who shared her Scandinavian good looks. "Leone was a kind soul, a lot of fun, hard working, a very good mother," recalled Caverly. "She wrote and sent photographs of [two-year-old] Mary Anne that I kept with my uniforms and personal things back on the submarine tender in Pearl Harbor."

Caverly was still in good physical condition from his boxing days before the war. But he was not the strongest of swimmers. The odds for survival seemed slim. *Would he see Mary Anne, Leone, and his folks again? Would he ever get to spend the $385 in poker winnings that he had locked away with the pictures of his family in Pearl Harbor?*[19]

IN THE WATER NEARBY, but out of sight, Captain Dick O'Kane also watched as the *Tang* went down, "the way a pendulum might swing down in a viscous liquid." His heart ached for the crew below the surface and for the few who had been topside and now had to face the cruel sea.

O'Kane could soon see the *Tang's* gray bow jutting above the surface at a forty-five-degree angle. The torpedo tubes were not exposed—there could be no escape through them. The *Tang* looked like "a great wounded animal, a leviathan." It was a devastating sight, far more wrenching than when he had heard of the *Wahoo's* loss. All he could feel was utter grief.[20] These moments would always haunt him, as would his memories of so many good men who were now dead, who had trusted him with their lives.[21]

O'Kane called out encouragement, as if trying to coax the *Tang* back to life. He then struck out instinctively toward his submarine, the first and only he had commanded. It was exhausting but he got closer, fighting the strong current. Every now and again, he saw a Japanese patrol boat in the far distance. It had not seen the *Tang* sink. Fortunately, her Mark 18 electric torpedoes had been wakeless, preventing the Japanese during the night's battle from immediately locating the *Tang*.

BILL LEIBOLD WAS NOT AS LUCKY—unlike Floyd Caverly and his captain, he was unable to step away in time from the bridge and swim clear of the sinking *Tang*. "I went down with the boat," he recalled. "I don't know how far but it seemed like it was a fair distance. I wasn't hanging onto anything. I was just standing there and all of a sudden I was submerged. I remember very clearly there was a distinct bump that made me start to swim back to the surface. It may have been when the stern hit the bottom. Or it could have been some kind of explosion."[22]

Leibold reached the surface. Regaining his composure, he heard men crying out. He recognized the voices of Chief Quartermaster Sidney Jones, his best friend aboard the *Tang*, and Gunner's Mate Darrell Rector from Kansas.[23] They were shouting to one another.

Leibold could feel himself being pulled away by the current. The voices grew fainter.

"Let's stay together," Leibold called out.[24]

There was no reply. Neither Jones nor Rector would ever be heard from again.

Leibold could not see anybody else in the water. He felt utterly alone. Then he noticed that the bow of the *Tang* was out of the water. As he swam toward it, he felt the sea push him back. It was soon clear that he would not make the bow because the current was too powerful. Then he saw the officer of the deck, Lieutenant John Heubeck, who had won swimming awards that he had pinned up in the *Tang*'s ward room. Heubeck was swimming the crawl expertly, and passed close by, headed for the bow. Then he was gone.

Leibold treaded water and tried to stay afloat, aware that he must conserve his energy. He knew he would have to get rid of anything that could weigh him down. So he threw away his binoculars, then his woolen jacket and shoes.

Leibold decided to keep his pants—they might save his life. He stripped them off, tied the legs, and tried to inflate them to make a life preserver. But no matter how he tied them, he couldn't manage to fill them with air.

Leibold had used up valuable energy trying to inflate the pants' legs. In frustration, he discarded them. He was left wearing nonregulation undershorts, with blue-and-white stripes, fastened by old-fashioned "ripper-snappers," and a thin dungaree shirt.

Leibold heard explosions. The Japanese were dropping depth charges somewhere not too far away. The Type 2 Model Z charges weighed around 350 pounds and had an explosive charge of around 230 pounds.[25] Leibold could feel the shock waves from the blasts. He couldn't see the boat that was dropping the charges though. It was pitch black. The depth-charging was intermittent: There were two or three explosions and then he would feel a small wave.

The Japanese eventually passed by and, once more, there was what seemed like dead silence.[26]

OUT OF LEIBOLD'S SIGHT and hearing, Floyd Caverly still struggled desperately to stay afloat. Suddenly, he spotted Lieutenant John Heubeck, who was still swimming confidently in a steady crawl. Caverly remembered that Heubeck was an award-winning swimmer at the Naval Academy. If any man could swim to safety, it was Heubeck.

"Is that you, Mr. Heubeck?" called Caverly.

Heubeck stopped swimming.

"Yes," said Heubeck. "Which way is land?"[27]

"About 180 feet straight down."[28]

Caverly was not certain in which direction land was. All he knew was that the China coast had been about ten miles to the west when the *Tang* had gone down. Since then he had been swimming in circles, carried by the current. It was dark. He was now completely disoriented.[29]

"Who are you?" Heubeck gasped.

"Caverly, sir."

"Which way is China?"

Caverly said he thought China was about ten miles to the west.

Heubeck set out for China. He was never seen again.

Caverly struggled once more to stay afloat. He had plenty of time for reflection, to think back on his adolescence, to the days before the war when one of his uncles in Minnesota had advised him to join the navy if hostilities broke out. At least in the navy, his uncle said, he would have a good meal every day. He wouldn't be stuck in a foxhole trying to keep his feet dry, eating C rations. And if he ever ended up in the water, his uncle added, he would only have to look out for himself.[30]

Stay afloat as long as you can, Caverly told himself.

There was no knowing how long he would have to wait until, perhaps, a Japanese boat picked up survivors . . . or until sharks attacked. One thing seemed certain: A long, dark night was ahead.

MEANWHILE, NOT FAR AWAY, O'Kane was also struggling to stay alive, also buoyed by thoughts of his family, and his thirty-two-year-old wife Ernestine. "I swam until I couldn't swim any more," recalled O'Kane. "Then I thought of Ernestine and swam some more."[31]

O'Kane had to stay focused. He had to concentrate on saving his energy—it was his only chance of one day seeing his strong-spirited Ernestine, whom he affectionately called his "boyhood chum," and their two small children, seven-year-old Marsha and five-year-old James, all of whom had been present at the launching of the *Tang.*

O'Kane had been a good father. Even as war raged across the Pacific, he had gotten to know his children, unlike many of his peers. He had spent as much time as possible with them. When he wasn't showing them around Mare Island submarine base, where Marsha got her hair cut by a navy barber, he took them on day trips to local towns and beaches, and to Yosemite National Park. It was on a visit with Marsha to bustling San Francisco that he bought a metronome for the *Tang* in a music store.[32]

O'Kane continued to tread water as he thought of his family. He was slowly losing strength. Then he felt a knock on his head. He turned around to discover a wooden door, debris from one of the ships he had sunk just hours before. The door could not hold all his weight, but it would help him stay afloat.

WHEN THE TORPEDO STRUCK, Larry Savadkin was standing beside the torpedo data computer in the conning tower, close to Radioman Edwin Bergman on the sonar. "The boat seemed to bounce up and down," he recalled. "I didn't lose my footing."[33]

Savadkin heard O'Kane ask if there was any propulsion and then moved away from the computer to check the pit log, which recorded the *Tang*'s speed.

The conning tower was plunged into utter darkness. Savadkin could sense the ocean gushing through the open hatch leading to the bridge. It had not been closed in time. He felt the *Tang* start to sink by the stern.

Water flooded the conning tower, threatening to drown him, Executive Officer Frank Springer, and six others who had been in the conning tower when the torpedo struck. Savadkin clung to the No. 2 periscope shaft.

Objects and drowning men swirled around him in a chaos of surging water.

What a hell of a way to die! thought Savadkin.[34]

But not just yet . . . twenty-four-year-old Savadkin had steady nerves and was supremely fit, having won awards as a middle-distance runner and never having smoked. O'Kane had noticed his cool head the first time Savadkin had taken the *Tang* down on her first dive on her third patrol.

A skinny, dark-haired, highly gifted engineer who grew up in Easton, Pennsylvania, and New York City, Savadkin had already distinguished himself in combat, having shown exceptional courage and sangfroid. Like Pete Narowanski, he served in the Mediterranean before attending submarine school. During the invasion of Sicily, he was wounded when German planes bombed his ship, the USS *Mayrant*, close to Palermo.

A bomb landed only a yard or two off the *Mayrant*'s port bow, rupturing her side and flooding her engineering room, where Savadkin had been working as the boat's engineering officer. Five men were killed and eighteen wounded in the attack, but the casualties would have been even greater had Savadkin and others not acted to save the *Mayrant* from sinking.

Savadkin was badly wounded in the head and traumatized as he watched men around him die. After recovering from his head wound at home in New York, he told his parents and teenage sister, Barbara, that he would rather go quickly next time, either in a plane or a submarine.[35] Because he couldn't fly, he opted for submarine duty. He was awarded the Silver Star for his prompt actions on July 26, 1943, as was his shipmate and friend, Lieutenant Franklin D. Roosevelt Jr., son of the president of the United States.

Savadkin now needed all the courage he could muster. Somehow, he found it, spurred by a fierce determination to again see his wife, whom he had known only briefly before leaving on the *Tang*. He also thought of his parents and sister. His mother, Esther, and father, Saul, had taught him, according to his sister Barbara, how to "roll with the punches, to accept that life is not a bed of roses, and to be practical and levelheaded under pressure."[36]

But nothing in his background could have prepared Savadkin for the nightmare he was now experiencing. The water had risen fast. In a matter of seconds, it was above his head.

Savadkin began to climb up the periscope. To his immense relief, he found an air bubble. He could fit his nose and mouth into it. It had formed in a small space where the periscope exited the hull, like some bead in an upturned carpenter's measure. He filled his lungs, his nose pressed against the *Tang*'s cork insulation.

There was utter silence. Savadkin had no idea where he was. He had completely lost his bearings. *Had the* Tang *flipped upside down? Which way should he go to try to escape?*

Savadkin filled his lungs again from the air bubble around the periscope. Treading water, he felt around in the blackness. Incredibly, his head popped into a larger air bubble. Then he touched something familiar—the engine room telegraph handle. He groped around some more. There was no doubting it—he could feel the ladder leading from the conning tower to the bridge. *Maybe, just maybe, there would be another air bubble above.* It was possible because the hatch to the bridge opened beneath cowling that might have trapped some air.

Filling his lungs again, Savadkin swam upward, out of the conning tower. It was pitch black. But luck was on his side—his hunch had been right—he found another air bubble below the cowling. Then, to his further amazement, Savadkin heard a voice. It belonged to Edwin Bergman. It sounded normal, not panicked.

Bergman had also groped his way out of the conning tower.[37]

"Who is it?" Bergman asked.

"Mr. Savadkin. Who are you?"

"Bergman. Do you know where we are?"

"I think we're under the bridge cowling."

"What are you going to do?"

Savadkin said he was going to try to swim to the surface.

"Can I come with you?"

"Sure."

"How?"

"Hold on to my legs."[38]

Bergman did so.

Savadkin filled his lungs with enough air, he hoped, to last a minute or so, and then struck out for the surface, "using both hands," as hard as he could.

Maybe Bergman was too afraid to make the terrifying ascent through the cold darkness. Or maybe he wanted to stay where he could at least breathe. In any case, he let go as Savadkin pushed upward. Like so many of the estimated forty men still alive in the *Tang*, he would never be seen again.

Savadkin figured he was at least fifty feet below the surface. The sea pressure was enormous but he was too focused on getting "air and lots of it" to notice.[39] He made sure he exhaled slowly so he didn't burst a lung. He was soon desperate for breath, on the verge of drowning, nearing the "break point": the moment at which chemical sensors in his brain would force him to take a breath, whether he wanted to or not.[40] Just as he thought he would have to "swallow some saltwater," he broke the surface and gasped the fresh air. He had done it. He was the first American to survive an ascent without breathing apparatus from a submarine.[41]

Savadkin looked around and saw the *Tang*'s anchor windlass. That meant the escape trunk in the forward torpedo room was submerged. If any men were still alive, there would be no easy way out.

Savadkin began to swim toward the *Tang*'s exposed bow. But he was in shock and exhausted from his ordeal in the conning tower. He needed to find something to hold him up—some piece of wreckage perhaps. But he could find nothing. Then he remembered his survival training at submarine school in San Diego, and how he had practiced using his pants to make a life preserver. It was fortunate that he was wearing long pants, unlike the other officers on the *Tang* who had preferred shorts while on duty in the tropics. He realized that he had lost his watch. His sandals had fallen off as he swam to the surface.

Savadkin removed his pants, tied them off, and began blowing. They slowly filled with air, enough to help keep him afloat. He alternated between floating on his front and his back. He soon felt cold and began to shiver uncontrollably, which made him swallow water.[42]

He had risen perhaps as much as 60 feet. It had almost killed him. What hope then for the men who were a farther 120 feet below? How could they survive without breathing apparatus? The *Tang* was surely too far down for any man to rise so far to the surface using only his own lungs?

Savadkin looked around in the darkness. No one was in sight. But he could see the gray bow of the *Tang* jutting above the sea, and far off he could make out another bow. It belonged to one of the *Tang*'s last victims.

Savadkin floated on his back. Bright stars were above. He heard the distant thuds of depth charges exploding, and a few seconds later he felt shock waves. He arched his back as they washed over him. Then he "screamed bloody murder," but there was no reply. Was he the lone survivor? It seemed that way.[43]

7

The Terrible Hours

CLAY DECKER WAS AT HIS BATTLE STATION on the bow planes in the *Tang's* control room, below the conning tower, when her last, erratic torpedo slammed into her. Luckily, he was sitting on a bench with a bulkhead at his back the moment the torpedo exploded. When the *Tang* was rocked by the resulting concussions, he was jarred only a few inches from where he was sitting. But others near him were thrown across the compartment. Decker saw two men fall through the hatch from the conning tower head first. One broke his neck; the other his back.

Decker could see men lying on the ruptured deck plates in agony, blood flowing from wounds inflicted as they were thrown against metal edges and machinery. Chief of the boat, Bill Ballinger, had been knocked out. Another man, John Accardy, had fallen through the hatch from the conning tower and broken his arm when he landed in the control room.[1] "I didn't get a bruise or a scratch even," recalled Decker. "But we had men who were in bad shape. [Ballinger] was thrown across the room and bashed across the bulkhead. Lieutenant Mel Enos also got banged up. He was bleeding from the forehead."[2]

Water was gushing down through the open hatch from the conning tower into the *Tang*'s control room. Decker saw several men trying to close it, but a wooden handle was caught in the closing mechanism.[3] The men could not seal the hatch properly, so water continued to rush in, though not as swiftly as before. Nevertheless, it was soon washing through the control room, seeping into the generators that powered the lighting. Decker and the other dozen or so men in the control room were cast into an eerie twilight.

Decker realized that the *Tang* was sinking by the stern—the compartment was tilting. It quickly settled at forty-five degrees. The bow was still out of the water, he figured, because he could hear waves sloshing against the hull. The *Tang*'s stern was no doubt stuck in the mud on the sea bottom. At least they had stopped sinking.

There was no time to lose. In a matter of minutes, Decker thought, the control room could be flooded and they would all drown. Tons of water had already gushed down into the submarine. It was clear to Decker that the rear compartments of the *Tang* were all flooded. At least half the crew, many of them close friends, had already drowned or been killed by the torpedo's explosion.

Determined not to share their fate, Decker began to focus on how to get out of the *Tang*. His best chance of survival lay in getting to the escape trunk in the forward torpedo room. But how were he and the other surviving men, several of them badly wounded, going to reach the trunk? Two sealed half-ton doors separated the control room from the forward torpedo room. Even if they could climb the forty-five degree angle upward, the men were not strong enough to open the doors held down by air pressure and gravity.

Decker realized that the only hope was to level the *Tang* so that he and his fellow survivors could then make their way through the submarine without having to climb up and lift hatch doors above them. To do that, they would have to sink the *Tang's* bow so that the submarine settled on the bottom.[4]

They would need a hydraulic jack to open the hatches and hydraulic pressure to flood the ballast tanks. But neither was available, making the task of leveling the *Tang* far more of a challenge but not impossible.

Decker kept a cool head. He had learned in submarine school that most of the hydraulic features on the boat had backups that could be operated by hand. Since joining the *Tang,* he had memorized the position of thousands of valves, levers, and switches. A long lever was attached to the overhead in the control room, above the chart table. If he could get to it, he would be able to manually flood the forward ballast tanks, thereby leveling the *Tang.* But time was running out—water continued to swamp the control room, rising inexorably.

Decker waded through the water and climbed onto the chart table. He lay on his back and reached up. There it was—the lever. He removed the safety pin and pulled on it with all his strength. Slowly, valves opened and tons of water poured into the forward ballast tanks. The *Tang* began to shift as the bow dropped gradually to the sea bottom.

Decker felt the bow finally settle down. There was a small jolt as she hit the bottom. Anyone who was still alive aboard the *Tang* was now 180 feet below the surface.

Survival was possible once more. Decker and others could at least move forward to the torpedo room. If they got there without mishap and in time, they could then try to escape through the small escape trunk.

JESSE DASILVA WAS IN the crew's quarters, to the aft of the control room, when the last torpedo was fired. The slight jolt as it left the *Tang* filled him with delight because they could now "head for the barn"—back to America. The tension began to ease in his face, although DaSilva knew he could only truly relax when the *Tang* was moored at the pier in Mare Island, across the bay from San Francisco. But now, at least, he would be moving away from danger rather than chasing it.⁵

Nineteen-year-old DaSilva had just been given a watch relief. Moving forward through the crew's quarters, he stopped in the air lock door between the bunkroom and the mess. Two men were nearby. One was sitting on a bunk with headphones on, listening to O'Kane's orders.

"All ahead emergency!"⁶

"Torpedo running circular!"⁷

The grins of just seconds ago disappeared. DaSilva could see in his crewmates' eyes a terrible foreboding. Each knew his life now hung in the balance. "The boyish face lines were forever erased in the blink of an eye," he recalled.⁸

DaSilva stepped into the mess area. It was then that the Mark 18 torpedo, carrying all 565 pounds of its Torpex load, hit the *Tang*.

He grabbed the ladder under the after battery hatch and held on tight as the *Tang* was "whipped around violently like a giant fish grabbed by the tail."[9]

Oh my God, what happened? thought DaSilva. *This is it. This is going to be the end. How long is it going to take?*[10]

When the reverberation stopped, DaSilva looked around in shock. Several men in the crew's quarters were badly hurt. The compartment to his rear—the forward engine room—was flooded. Looking forward, DaSilva could see water streaming over the sill connecting the crew's mess, where he stood, to the control room.

DaSilva and two other men acted fast, trying to shut the half-ton door that connected the compartments. It was very difficult to do so. They had to push against the oncoming water and high-pressure air. Then DaSilva felt the deck tilt upwards.

The *Tang* was sinking. That much was obvious. It was soon impossible to stand upright without support.

DaSilva hung on as men around him slipped and fell aft. He felt the *Tang*'s stern touch down on the sea floor. Air in the scaled compartments at the fore of the boat had clearly kept the bow above the surface. That was something, at least. "It was as if the *Tang* herself was trying to breathe the life-giving air," DaSilva recalled, "and hold on as long as she could."[11]

"The boat acted as a thoroughbred," recalled one of the other men, "dying but still trying to save the crew."[12]

ON THE SURFACE, Dick O'Kane saw the *Tang*'s bow disappear beneath the surface.

Surely, that was no accident?

It looked as if someone inside the *Tang* had flooded a ballast tank to level the *Tang* on the bottom.

Some of his men were alive.

That had to be the case. If they were, they would now at least have a fighting chance.

O'Kane watched the surface where the *Tang* had been, hoping for some sign of life from the boat. *Perhaps the escape buoy will appear?* Time passed. But he saw nothing, and soon the current pushed him away from the area.[13]

AROUND 180 FEET BELOW, the men near DaSilva picked themselves up and got back to the task at hand: closing the half-ton door between the crew's mess and the control room. If they didn't get it shut fast, they would drown.[14]

DaSilva grasped the door and pulled. The heavy hatch wouldn't budge. But he and others were now so pumped with adrenaline, so desperate to live, that they somehow summoned immense strength. Inch by inch, they forced it shut.

Wide-eyed with relief, DaSilva and his buddies looked at each other.[15] They all knew what they had done. They had saved themselves from drowning—for the time being—but in the process they had locked themselves into a compartment that had no escape trunk.[16] Moreover, only a flimsy deck separated them from 120 storage batteries under their feet. It would take just one leakage of water into just one battery for deadly chlorine gas to form.[17]

If more water got into more batteries, more gas would form and then slowly, imperceptibly at first, it would begin to kill them, bleaching their lungs until they finally choked to death. "There were about twenty of us in the crew's quarters and the mess," remembered DaSilva. "We knew that we couldn't remain there long because of chlorine gas from the flooded batteries."[18]

Chlorine gas had been the stuff of submariners' nightmares ever since men trapped in a submerged German U-boat had survived to tell of its devastating effect in a confined space with no ventilation. In 1915, the *U-57* had hit a mine off the coast of Scotland, sinking to 128 feet with twenty men on board. Seawater quickly flooded the submarine's batteries, resulting in chlorine gas filling the boat. Men's ears ached intolerably as the pressure grew. Soon they could scarcely breathe as the chlorine fumes scorched their lungs. Frantically, the crew looked for breathing apparatus but could find only four units. When the pain had become unbearable, two men picked up pistols and shot themselves to death.

Jesse DaSilva did not want to die of chlorine poisoning. They could not stay where they were. Their only chance of survival was to get to the forward torpedo room, which had the escape trunk. "But we had to go through the control room to get there," recalled DaSilva.[19]

"We'll just have to take a chance and see if the control room is flooded or not," someone said.

Suddenly, there were the distant thuds of depth charges. Surely, with the *Tang* crippled, her bow jutting above the surface providing an excellent target, they would soon be blown to hell by a Japanese shell?

MEANWHILE, IN THE forward torpedo room, about ten men had gathered. They knew that they were close to the surface because they could hear the sound of waves slapping against the *Tang*'s hull. They also knew that there were only two ways out of the *Tang*: through the escape trunk or through the torpedo tubes. Both were daunting routes to survival.

Someone suggested that they try to get out through the forward torpedo tubes, not realizing that they were submerged. It was not as crazy as it sounded. Men had managed it before when they had escaped the fabled *S-48*, the unluckiest submarine in U.S. naval history.

On December 7, 1921, on her very first test dive, the *S-48* had sunk to the bottom of Long Island Sound with forty-one men aboard. Someone had forgotten to replace a faulty manhole cover on her stern ballast tank and the *S-48* had plunged rapidly and settled sixty feet from the surface, with three after compartments flooded. Fortunately, her quick-thinking captain had ordered the closing of watertight hatches, sealing off the flooded compartments. Then he had blown the forward ballast tanks with air at full pressure and managed to at least raise the bow far enough above the surface that the torpedo tube exits were exposed. Realizing this, the captain had ordered his men to get out of the *S-48* through the tubes. Every one of his crew survived.[20]

Could the *Tang*'s crew also squeeze their way through tubes and live to tell the tale? Only those slim enough to fit through the *Tang*'s twenty-one-inch wide tubes would be able to do so with ease. Few of the men were sufficiently skinny, given the always available supply of superb food aboard the *Tang*. Those with thicker waistlines would have no option but to try the escape trunk attached to the bulkhead above them.

Suddenly, the men in the forward torpedo room could hear the distant thuds and reverberations of Japanese depth charges. Like the men trapped in other compartments, they now wondered how long it would take before the Japanese spotted the *Tang*'s exposed bow and opened fire with surface guns.[21]

Then the deck below them started to shift and in consternation they felt the *Tang* begin to level off and settle to the bottom. They couldn't use the torpedo tubes now in any case. There was just one way out—the escape trunk.

JESSE DASILVA KNEW he had to keep moving forward or die. He and several others were gathered at the door sealing the crew's quarters from the control room. Looking through the eye port, they could see that, although the control room was badly flooded, the water had not yet entered the ventilation piping. It was likely that the control room still had some air in it, which meant they could risk opening the door.

But first DaSilva and the men trapped with him decided to prepare for the inevitable rush of water when they opened the door. DaSilva lifted some decking and opened a freezer locker below it so that it would act as a makeshift bilge and collect at least some of the water. A storeroom and the *Tang*'s magazine were also below the decking. At some point, Gunner's Mate James White had emptied the magazine of firearms to take forward to the torpedo room.[22]

DaSilva and the others climbed onto oblong tables. The tables had raised sides to prevent plates from sliding to the deck and were patterned with checkerboard squares.

Someone cracked open the door. Dirty water gushed in. Tense moments followed as the crew's mess filled with the overspill. *Would the water continue to rush in or subside?* To their relief, it leveled after a few seconds. The men climbed down from the mess tables and waded through water that began to settle around their ankles.

About a dozen men, including DaSilva, started to make their way into the control room.[23] It was soon clear that the room had partly flooded because of water that was still leaking into it from the damaged hatch leading to the flooded conning tower above.

The men waded through the control room toward the officer's mess. The water was soon reaching their knees.

DaSilva looked around the control room. He spotted Mel Enos, the eager young officer of whom O'Kane had expected great things. "We'd better destroy some of these papers," said Enos.

Enos was still bleeding from several deep cuts to his head.[24] He began showing men which vital documents to destroy. Some of the men began to carry out his orders without thinking, setting fire to codebooks and other confidential documents, including top secret Ultra messages, which were held in a safe in the wardroom or in another safe in the captain's stateroom nearby.

As an officer, Enos had access to both safes and he knew the importance of the information inside because he had decoded key Ultra messages in recent weeks. In the dimly lit room, DaSilva could make out documents piled up in a wastebasket set on a table.

Enos set fire to them, creating a "great deal of smoke."[25] It was a stupid thing to do in a sunken submarine with a fast dwindling oxygen supply. But he wasn't thinking straight. He was a green ensign. Before joining the *Tang*, he had never even been to sea.[26]

Other men, led by Doc Larson, began to carry injured crew members forward, using blankets as litters.

"We've got to get to the forward torpedo room because that's where we can make an escape," someone said.

From the control room, they stepped into the adjacent officers' quarters.

As Jesse DaSilva moved forward, he noticed that the high-pressure air tank was full. He felt a jolt of hope. They had air. It would not last long, but a couple of hours' supply was left at the least.[27]

They would need every breath they could get. Already the *Tang*'s normally thick fog of body odor, diesel fumes, and stale air was starting to become difficult to breathe. There was also the steady buildup of carbon dioxide from the rapidly exhaled breath of the men. Many of them were probably already panting because of increased heart rates due to shock and the adrenaline pumping through them.

To compound the problem, at 180 feet below, the air was under far higher pressure than on the surface, and this meant there would be a far greater increase in carbon dioxide when exhaling. Sooner or later, the men literally could be killed by their own breath.

DaSilva kept moving. He saw three apple pies that had been laid out on tables, no doubt for the crew to celebrate on their return to San Francisco. Others noticed turkeys that were thawing for the Thanksgiving dinner that was to have been held on their journey home.[28]

DaSilva continued forward. He spotted a depth gauge. It showed that the *Tang* was at 180 feet. That was deep, but not too deep to rule out a successful exit from the forward torpedo room's escape trunk. Had they sunk in several hundred feet of water, there would now be no chance of survival. The best option, in that case, would be to put a pistol to one's head.

OTHER MEN WERE also working their way toward the forward torpedo room. Clay Decker stuck close to chief Bill Ballinger, who had recovered somewhat from being thrown across the compartment when the *Tang*'s last torpedo struck. As the pair passed through the officer's mess, they also encountered the young junior-grade lieutenant, Mel Enos. He was still busy burning codebooks and other papers in the metal wastebasket.

"You can't do that, Enos, you can't do that!" cried Decker. "We can't have a fire going! We need every bit of air we've got!"[29]

Enos stopped setting light to the codebooks.

Decker and Ballinger grabbed the remaining codebooks, dropped below into the forward battery compartment and dunked them into the battery acid, a far safer and instantaneous method of disposal.

As many as twenty survivors continued forward through the submarine. It was around 2:45 a.m., fifteen minutes or so after the torpedo had struck, when they reached a sealed door—all that separated them from the forward torpedo room. Among the men who gathered before the door were Mel Enos, Clay Decker, Bill Ballinger, Doc Larson, Hank Flanagan, and Jesse DaSilva. The more experienced among them, and those who were still thinking relatively clearly, in spite of the oxygen-depleted air, knew that they now faced a serious problem.

The difference in air pressure between the forward torpedo room and the compartment they were in was likely to be enormous. If they opened the door without attempting to equalize the pressure between the two compartments, they could be shot forward like pellets in an air gun.

To make matters worse, on close examination, the men realized that the intercom linking the two compartments wasn't working. Soon, men on both sides of the door were trying to tell each other what they planned, gesturing at each other through the eye port and hammering on the door. Chaos ensued. No one on either side had a clear idea of what the other group was about to do next. Banging on the door—any kind of unnecessary noise—was a bad idea. In fact, it was life-threatening given the presence of sonar-equipped Japanese patrol boats that were trying to locate the *Tang*.

In the forward torpedo room, Hayes Trukke saw that high-pressure air lines had snapped, no doubt when the torpedo had struck. That meant there was not just a significant but a massive difference in air pressure between the two compartments.

Trukke urgently attempted to signal to DaSilva and others that they should open the door very slowly.[30] But it was no use. The men standing near DaSilva on the other side of the sealed door began to panic, terrified that they would be trapped in a compartment with no way out. Thinking that Trukke and others were trying to keep them out, they started to push against the door with all their brute strength. Suddenly, it seemed to explode. The men were blown forward.[31]

In the forward torpedo room Howard Walker felt the full brunt of the door suddenly bursting open, hitting him in the face. Hayes Trukke saw that Walker's nose was squashed to one side, his "lips smashed and eyes closed."[32] Blood poured from the wound.[33] Doc Larson did his best to patch him up.

Finally, Jesse DaSilva and the men with him entered the forward torpedo room. Most of the men were familiar with the compartment, and had fond memories of it, having visited it most evenings to watch movies such as *Dracula* and *Flying Down to Rio,* which were projected onto a screen at one end.

The air inside was worse than in the compartments they had left behind: dense with minute debris and so full of exhaled carbon dioxide that it was hard for every man gathered there to breathe normally. And it was hot, above one hundred degrees Fahrenheit and getting hotter by the second—without ventilation, heat from the engines and other sources had no outlet.

DaSilva figured that about forty men, some seriously injured, were now in the forward torpedo compartment.[34] They were "excited, scared and didn't know what to do."[35]

CLAY DECKER WAS ASTONISHED to see his best friend, Motor Machinist's Mate George Zofcin, among the white-faced survivors in the forward torpedo room. "When we had gone to battle stations submerged," he recalled, "I had left the throttles to George and gone to the control room. I figured he was back [in the engine room in the after part of the boat] when we took the torpedo. I was absolutely flabbergasted when I got to the forward torpedo room and saw George."[36]

Zofcin told Decker that he had stepped away from his position in the engine room after the last torpedo had been fired and moved forward toward the galley to get a cup of coffee. He had been standing just a few feet from the galley when the last torpedo hit the *Tang*.

"Then I just stepped through the hatch and closed it behind me," Zofcin told an astonished Decker.

Twenty-one-year-old George Zofcin and Clay Decker were particularly close. They met in San Francisco, where Zofcin had grown up, during the commissioning of the *Tang*. Like Decker, the light-haired, boyish-looking Zofcin was married to an attractive young woman, Martha, and like Decker, he had a two-year-old son. Zofcin approached Decker as soon as he learned from other crewmen that Decker and he had sons the same age.

The two men often discussed their wives and sons with each other. Decker told Zofcin that his wife, Lucille, was working at a Bay Area shipyard as a secretary when she wasn't caring for his son, Harry.

"I've also got a wife and a two-year-old son," Zofcin told Decker. "I just bought a house over at 67 Stonyford Avenue on the hill in San Francisco. It's as small as a postage stamp. You step off the sidewalk and two strides later you're in the front door. But the back yard is big enough for a small picnic table and two chairs. It's a two bedroom with two stories. Just my wife and son are going to be there when I go aboard the *Tang* and make this patrol."

"Maybe your wife and mine could live together," Zofcin suggested. "Your wife can bring in the beans. Mine can look after the children."[37]

The arrangement was working out perfectly so far.

ALSO AMONG THE MEN in the forward torpedo room was the muscle-bound Leland Weekley, the chief torpedoman. An avid bodybuilder who lifted weights in the forward torpedo room when not on duty there, Weekley had complained to Floyd Caverly and others that his marriage to his wife, Edith, who was living in Compton in Los Angeles, had been under strain for a while. But he had recently received a letter from her, which had filled him with the hope of patching things up. As much as any other man, he was now determined to get out of the *Tang* so that he could be with loved ones again.

Weekley stepped onto a ladder and climbed the few feet to a hatch on the overhead. Then he opened it and looked up into the *Tang*'s escape trunk.[38] Below him, men began to pull out cellophane-wrapped Momsen Lungs that had been stowed in overheads. As they did so, some discussed the odds of getting out of the *Tang* alive, and what they would do if they got to the surface. They knew how deep they were and roughly how far it was to the coast of China. At this point, they were all confident they would survive.[39]

Suddenly, the men could hear depth charges exploding far off. Invaluable time passed as they waited for the depth-charging to end, their faces taut with tension, sweat streaming off their brows. Never had an escape been attempted from a submerged submarine while under attack. "Jap patrol boats [had] evidently picked us up again," recalled one of the men, "and dropped about ten depth charges, which shook us severely but did no real damage. Everything came to a dead standstill until they had left and there was no danger of them picking up our sounds."[40]

Finally, the Japanese patrol boats moved away. The men continued to distribute the Momsen Lungs, breathing devices that theoretically enabled a man to rise from depths of up to three hundred feet to the surface without being killed by the bends.[41] Without the Lungs, the men in the *Tang*'s forward torpedo room believed they were doomed.

The Momsen Lung was an ingenious device. Valves allowed exhaled air to flow into a foot-square breathing bag, where it was enriched with oxygen. The air was then inhaled through a container of soda lime, which stripped the air of potentially lethal carbon dioxide. A more recent refinement to the apparatus was the addition of a nose-clip to make sure the man wearing it breathed in and out through a mouthpiece. The nose-clip could be fixed to a pair of goggles. A valve regulated air pressure behind the goggles' lens so that men could clear their vision.

It was soon obvious that some of the men were having problems fitting their Momsen Lung. Most of them had not been trained properly in how to use it. Their brains were slowly being starved of oxygen and so the device must have seemed infuriatingly complex. Even those who had used it before in training had never tried it again, figuring that if they ever went down, it would be in water below three hundred feet, and that was too deep for the Lung to be of any use. Throughout the Silent Service it was generally assumed that no one would survive a sinking, and many crew, and not a few captains, had resented the valuable space taken up by the Momsen Lungs.

One thing now seemed clear: Being able to use the Momsen Lung effectively, or rather without making a mistake, would soon decide who lived and who died. The stakes were the highest possible. And there was no precedent to give comfort. No American had yet gotten out of a sunken submarine alive without assistance from the surface.[42]

The only possible comparison with the *Tang*'s current fate was the situation faced by the survivors aboard the USS *S-51* back in 1925. The *S-51* had gone down in 132 feet of water—50 less than the *Tang*'s current depth. Thirty-three men were alive as the *S-51* settled to the bottom.

None survived.[43]

JESSE DASILVA LOOKED AROUND. He and the other survivors were crammed into the forward torpedo room, a semicircular space that was thirty feet long. Chief Pharmacist's Mate Paul Larson did what he could to treat the wounded as men donned their Momsen Lungs. Fortunately, he had found extra medical supplies in an emergency store in the torpedo room.

The air continued to get worse. It was increasingly hard to see: The emergency lights grew weaker as more water dripped into the batteries and cells shorted.[44] Every few minutes, the lights dimmed, went out, and then shone feebly again.[45]

Lieutenant Mel Enos thought it might still be possible to escape from the *Tang* through a gun-access hatch back in the control room. Others agreed that this was a reasonable idea. Enos gathered six volunteers. Someone opened the door leading back toward the control room. There was a "terrific blast" of black smoke that smelt like burnt rubber. The smoke streamed into the forward torpedo room, completely filling it, forcing men to cough and gag. The door was quickly closed. A fire was in another compartment. That was certain. Its smoke was so toxic that cracking the door open for just a second had made some of the men vomit. And now there was so much of the smoke in the room that the emergency lights were "dim glows."[46]

Enos and his party gave up on getting back to the control room: It had been another bad idea—another rash move, as with the burning of codebooks—that had only made matters worse. The air in the torpedo room was now so poisoned from burning rubber and other chemicals that some men started to use their Momsen Lung just to stop suffocating. Others were already starting to fade, their brains addled by the lack of oxygen and a lethal combination of heat, carbon dioxide, and toxic fumes.

THE MEN WERE NOW TRAPPED in the forward torpedo room. It was already 3 a.m., high time they made a move. Twenty-eight-year-old Lieutenant Hank Flanagan, with twelve years in the navy, assumed command and began to organize the first escape attempt.

The prospect of making the ascent unnerved many of the men.[47] They had all, at some point, wondered what they would do if the worst happened and they found themselves trapped as they were now. There were three options—escape, die slowly from lack of oxygen, or put a .45 caliber pistol to your head to bring the living nightmare to an end.[48] Which would it be? Every man would have to decide for himself.

There was a delay organizing the first escape group while some men had second thoughts and argued about whether the escape trunk was really their only way out. Some men suggested it would be a good idea to fire men from a torpedo tube. Flanagan dismissed the idea immediately: It would be lethal, not least because of the difference in pressure between the torpedo tube and the outside waters.

Finally, at about 3:15 a.m., the first group of four began to gather. But only then was a major problem discovered that would complicate the escape trunk's use. Air lines were broken, so they would not be able to blow the water from the trunk after it had been used. They would need to drain the water into a bilge in the forward torpedo room.

In the meantime, Gunner's Mate James White, a married man from Louisiana, stepped forward. He had an armful of web belts and several .45 pistols. He had brought them from the arsenal below the decking in the crew's mess so that every man could put one on. He began to distribute the guns and some knives.

"We knew that we would be going into shark-infested water," Decker confirmed later. "White brought enough side arms for every man to have a .45. We also had shells, which we wrapped in gauze and paper and stuck in our pockets, and C-rations. We unbuttoned our fly and tied the rations to our legs with our shoe strings."[49]

Armed with rations and weapons, several of the men gathered at the steps to the escape trunk and began discussing how best to operate it, knowing that one mistake could possibly doom every other survivor in the torpedo room.

Four men would enter the small escape trunk, which was connected by a hatch to the torpedo room. In the trunk were gauges, indicating depth and pressure inside and out, and an oxygen outlet from which to fill the Momsen Lung. When the men had gathered in the trunk, they would allow seawater to pour into it until the pressure was higher inside the trunk than the sea outside. The seawater would then stop pouring in and the men could open a door leading to the outside. The men would then fill their Momsen Lung with oxygen. To guide them through the dark waters to the surface, they would release a yellow wooden buoy, the size of a soccer ball, attached to a five hundred-foot-long line knotted every ten feet.

The men would follow the line up, pausing at each knot so that they did not rise more than fifty feet per minute. This slow ascent, although counterintuitive to any man wanting to reach the surface, was crucial to survival because it allowed a man to adjust to decreasing pressure as he rose, thereby avoiding decompression sickness, more commonly known as the bends. Under high pressure, nitrogen is absorbed into the bloodstream in much higher quantities than at sea level. As a result, if a diver or escaping submariner rises to the surface too quickly, the nitrogen expands in his bloodstream and forms intensely painful bubbles. The effect is usually deadly if a man rises too fast from significant depths, the nitrogen bubbles acting rather like the bubbles in a shaken can of soda when it is opened suddenly.

From 180 feet down, their ascent should in theory take between three to four minutes. Timing was everything. They must rise slowly, but not too slowly, inhaling at each knot and exhaling slowly as they rose to the next. If they did not exhale, the air pressure in their lungs would increase massively as they ascended, leading to a possible burst lung, which was often fatal.

After the last man had exited, he would bang on the trunk— the signal for the escape door to be closed by a lever from inside the torpedo room. Then the seawater would be allowed to drain into the bilges and another four men would take their place in the escape trunk. Unfortunately, because of the Japanese patrol boats above, banging on the trunk placed the men in a terrible double bind. The only way they could communicate with the men waiting their turn was by banging, and yet the sound was bound to give away the *Tang*'s position to the enemy at some point.[50] It seemed that they were doomed if they didn't and doomed if they did.

In the training manuals, the escape procedure had seemed straightforward enough, but in practice it was anything but simple—as the men were about to find out. As one of the survivors would later put it: "An escape procedure is very simple on paper but somewhat different when everyone's life depends on it."[51]

Howard Walker, the black steward, listened as the men discussed how to use the trunk.

Walker was seated on a step, having had his busted nose and lips treated by Doc Larson. He was probably not in much pain because Larson had also found morphine spikes in the emergency store in the forward torpedo room.

"A lot of praying and a little less talk would do us all a lot of good," said Walker.[52]

IT WAS 3:30 A.M., about an hour after the sinking. Men in the first escape group began to climb the ladder into the escape trunk. The most bullish among them was twenty-year-old Mel Enos, the only child of a couple from Vallejo, where the *Tang* had been built.[53] "He had loaded himself down with two .45s strapped to his waist, two bandoliers of ammunition, and a knife, and had filled his shorts with chocolate bars and food," recalled one of the survivors. "He was all set on reaching China."[54]

Enos was joined by Torpedoman John Fluker, a Virginian, and the wily "sea dog," chief Bill Ballinger. Standard procedure was for four men to get into the trunk, but now they decided that a rubber life raft should take the place of a fourth man. It may help them survive if they ever reached the surface.

Men below closed the hatch to the escape trunk. Fluker, Enos, Ballinger, and the life raft were sealed inside the small trunk, crushed together with barely enough room to stand. Precious minutes were again wasted as they disagreed on how to rig the trunk.[55] Finally, one of them cranked a valve that allowed seawater into the trunk. Doing so was a giant leap of faith. In theory, the water would rush in until it reached their chests, raising the pressure inside the trunk so that it equalized the external pressure of the water at 180 feet below. But none of the men could be sure that it would stop at their chests. What if it didn't?

The seawater gushed in, past their ankles, toward their waists. As more poured in and the pressure increased, the men found it hard to endure. It was difficult to breathe. They were soon panting. The escape trunk was acting like a piston chamber as the water rose. The temperature soared, making them sweat profusely and causing their hearts to race. Keeping one's nerve was close to impossible. They were jammed together like sardines and one man's confusion and panic badly affected the others. The simplest procedure—such as attaching the buoy to a reel of escape line—was a nerve-wracking challenge.[56]

The strain was too much. Enos was the first to crack. He did not wait for the buoy to be tied to the escape line and released. As soon as the door was opened, he dived out.[57] It was a fatal mistake. The door did not lead directly to the ocean. It opened instead to the submarine's superstructure. Without an escape line to guide him, a man could easily get lost in the darkness. And that is what probably happened to Enos. It is thought that he got stuck in the space between the hull and the deck, weighed down by his weapons.

According to one survivor, men in the torpedo room below heard a frantic clanging and banging as Enos searched in vain for a way out. Then there was a haunting silence. Enos had apparently drowned, killed perhaps as much by his youth and haste as by the water.[58]

Meanwhile, back in the escape trunk, Ballinger and Fluker argued about how best to get out and how to release the buoy. If they made a mistake, they could endanger the men remaining below them in the torpedo room. They had to get this right.

Forty minutes had passed since Enos and the others had entered the trunk. To those waiting in the torpedo room for their turn to escape, it felt like an eternity. "Under the conditions," recalled Pete Narowanski, "a minute was just like an hour."[59]

Unwilling to waste any more time, Hank Flanagan pulled on the lever operating the trunk's external door, thereby closing it, and drained the trunk. When the hatch to the escape trunk was then opened, the men saw an exhausted Bill Ballinger and John Fluker. Mel Enos had disappeared. The rubber boat was still in the trunk.

When they were lowered back down into the forward torpedo room, Ballinger said he wanted to try again. But Fluker was worn out, and said he would have to recuperate before making another attempt. The sight of the two men, clearly traumatized by their experience in the trunk, was deeply depressing to the men in the torpedo room hoping to stay alive.[60] Death seemed to step closer.

8

Blow and Go

THE SKY BEGAN TO LIGHTEN. **Dawn beckoned.**

    Bill Leibold alternated between swimming the breast stroke and floating on his back. The minutes, then hours, had passed slowly. Leibold had lost sense of time. The water felt cold. "No doubt about it," he would recall sixty-three years later, "the thought of my wife during that long swim was a strong factor in surviving."[1]

It had been ten months since Leibold had last seen his nine-teen-year-old wife, Grace. She was a funny, spirited blonde, the sweetest woman he had ever met. They had attended the same high school. She had been serious about getting good grades while Leibold had been far more interested in submarines and the navy. After the war broke out, they had written to each other frequently.

They dated just two or three times before they were married and had spent only four months together as man and wife. But those months, sharing a three-bedroom apartment with another newly married couple in navy housing on Mare Island, had been pure bliss.

Grace had been under the impression that he would stay ashore as master of arms in the shipyard administration office at Mare Island. To avoid upsetting her, Leibold had "fibbed" to her about joining the *Tang,* saying he had been drafted when in fact he had done all he possibly could to get aboard.[2] She had returned to live with her parents in Los Angeles when the *Tang* left for the Pacific on its first patrol on January 1, 1944, and now worked as a stenographer in the Probate Department of the Los Angeles Superior Court. It was a good job and kept her busy. Maybe keeping busy would help her deal with the news that the *Tang* had disappeared, presumed lost with all hands. . . .

Leibold heard the sound of splashing and spluttering.

Floyd Caverly could also hear someone or *something* splashing about. He looked around. Like Leibold, he couldn't see anything, but he knew he was in shark-infested waters.

"Who's there?" cried Caverly.

"Leibold."

"Come on over here," said Caverly.

"Over where?" replied Leibold. "I don't know where you're at."

Caverly kept talking and Leibold moved toward his voice. It wasn't long before they found each other.[3]

Leibold could see that Caverly was struggling to keep his head above water as he tried to float on his back. He was gasping for air and being swamped by each wave.

"You're not going to leave me out in this dark ocean all alone," Leibold told Caverly, trying to encourage him.

Caverly said he was having trouble keeping his head above water.

Leibold watched him for a few moments.

"Cav, when you feel your head come up and then start down," Leibold instructed him, "you're through the wave. Your head is then out of the water—that's when you take a breath of air."

Caverly followed Leibold's advice.

"Hey, that works pretty damn good," said Caverly. "Are you doing it?"

"No. But now that I've explained it to you, and it works, I think I'll do it too."[4]

Leibold and Caverly stuck close together, helping each other. Every now and then, Caverly swallowed a mouthful of water and then spat it out. Both felt increasingly cold. They knew they were losing precious body heat when they began to shiver. The first stages of hypothermia were setting in. The water was probably no more than fifty degrees Fahrenheit in this part of the Formosa Strait in late October. Men had been known to die in as little as three to four hours in similar conditions.

This time it was Caverly who had the smart idea: He told Leibold they should turn into the current and then urinate. Their urine would warm them. Caverly was right. It wasn't long before they were urinating regularly to fend off the cold.[5]

Leibold and Caverly decided to wait until daylight and then try to get to the exposed bow of one of the ships sunk by the *Tang*. There was bound to be something there that they could latch onto, and then they could use the current to wash them toward an island or the coast of China. Just before the *Tang* had gone down, Caverly had gotten a range reading—the nearest land had been an island off the coast of China called Fouchow, some twenty thousand yards away.

Dawn was nigh. Light soon streaked the sky. As day broke, Leibold and Caverly spotted what they thought was land. When they looked again, they realized it had been a mirage—it was only a cloud.

IN THE *Tang*'s forward torpedo room 180 feet below, Hank Flanagan, the last remaining officer, decided to take charge of a second escape attempt. It was around 4:15 a.m. when he started to organize the next party. This time, the rubber boat would be jettisoned to make room for a fourth man.[6]

Determined to try again, Bill Ballinger asked for volunteers to join him and Flanagan.

"I'm going to go," said Ballinger. "I need volunteers."

Clay Decker stepped forward. He knew Ballinger was the most experienced submariner among the survivors. He had completed six runs on the USS *Tunney* before he had come aboard the *Tang* for her first patrol, and had been the main conduit between O'Kane and the crew. More than any other man still alive, he had a natural authority that inspired confidence.

Ballinger also had a salty sense of humor. He cursed royally, drove the crew hard, but could also be great fun when he was relaxing, which was rare given his responsibilities on the *Tang*. He had grown up in California. About five foot ten inches, with "dark hair and strong features," Ballinger had earned the crew's respect as chief of the boat but also as the *Tang*'s leading torpedoman, responsible for the men in both forward and after torpedo rooms.

Already, at least half of the mostly teenage boys under his charge were dead: Phillip Anderson from Grand Rapids; Fred Bisogno, an Italian from Brooklyn; Wilfred Boucher from Rhode Island; John

Foster from Detroit; Texan William Galloway; and Charles Wadsworth from California. At least none of them had been married.

Decker stepped toward Ballinger.

I'm going to get on his shirttail, thought Decker. *He knows where he's going.*

"I'm with you, Bill," said Decker.[7]

Soon, five men had gathered at the steps leading to the trunk: Ensign Basil Pearce from Florida, Bill Ballinger, Hank Flanagan, Leland Weekley, and Clay Decker.[8]

Decker picked up his Momsen Lung and ripped open its celluloid packaging. His close friend, George Zofcin, helped him put on the lung. In the flickering light, Zofcin noticed that the clip on the lung's discharge valve was still attached. He removed it, not knowing then that this simple action probably saved Decker's life.

Decker hustled Zofcin toward the escape trunk, urging him to join the attempt.

"No, no," Zofcin said.

"Come on, let's get our asses outta here, George," said Decker.

"No, no, Clay, you go ahead and go with this wave."

"Why George? Come on, go with us."

"No. No . . . I've got a confession to make."

"Confessions? What the hell are we talking about? We've got to get our butts off of this boat."

"Clay, I can't swim."

Decker was dumbfounded. He couldn't believe it. How could Zofcin not swim? If there was one thing every submariner could do, it was swim.

Back in Hawaii, before setting out on the *Tang's* last patrol, Decker and Zofcin had shared a room at the Royal Hawaiian for two weeks; they had visited Waikiki beach in their swimsuits several times. Zofcin had never gone into the water.

Decker said it didn't matter whether Zofcin could swim or not.

"Look, George," added Decker, pointing to his Momsen Lung. "You can use it as a life preserver. . . . You can also hang on to the buoy that's at the end of the line."[9]

Zofcin was not convinced.

"Clay, you go now," he said. "I'll go with the next wave."[10]

Decker felt torn. He didn't want to leave Zofcin behind. How would he explain to Zofcin's young wife, Martha, that he had made it but Zofcin had been too afraid to try?

But time was running out if he was to follow Ballinger into the escape trunk and stand a chance of surviving and seeing his own family again. Reluctantly, Decker turned away and climbed up the ladder leading to the escape trunk.

Hank Flanagan was standing nearby. He watched Decker get into the trunk. He also saw Zofcin walk over to a bunk and crawl into it, apparently resigned to dying in the *Tang*.

Zofcin soon appeared to fall asleep. He was one of several men who were now so terrified of the escape procedure and so drained by exhaustion and the increasing heat and toxic fumes that they were unwilling to save themselves.[11]

A few seconds later, Decker, Ballinger, Flanagan, and Pearce were squeezed together in the escape trunk. It was around 4:15 a.m. when the trunk was sealed from below. "It was a small space," recalled Decker. "There was battery lighting in the escape chamber itself. It wasn't very bright but we could see what we were doing. The four of us were standing almost nose-to-nose. There was a fathometer, which showed 180 feet, and a pressure gauge that showed the external pressure outside the hull."[12]

The men started to fill the trunk with water. It was soon up to their shins. When it reached above their waists, Ballinger and Decker tested their Momsen Lungs by ducking under the water briefly. The pressure became more intense the higher the water rose. The men began to lose their senses. The pressure was soon so high—ninety pounds per square inch—that they could barely hear each other; normal air pressure is six times less at fifteen pounds per square inch. When they spoke, their voices squeaked, as if they had gulped helium rather than oxygen from their Momsen Lungs.

In the forward torpedo room below the escape trunk, men again waited impatiently. There was no means of communication with the men in the escape trunk other than by tapping on the bulkhead—a major design flaw in the escape system.

Back in the escape trunk, aches and pains stabbed the men's ears. Eventually, the water was up to their chests. Because Decker was shorter then the others, the water actually reached his neck.[13]

The men's heads were in an air bubble. They then bled compressed air into the air bubble and, in agony and close to passing out, watched until a gauge showed that the pressure in the trunk exceeded the sea pressure outside by five pounds. That would, in theory, enable them to open the hatch with no strain, just like opening a door to a room in a house.

Clay Decker had long since resigned himself to the inevitability of dying if the *Tang* sank. "Every night you laid your head on your pillow," recalled Decker, "you were aware that the piece of iron that's a submarine could end up being a tomb." Now, with a chance at life, Decker was afraid but able to control his panic. Others in the escape trunk reacted differently, as if the gravity of their situation paralyzed them with trepidation.

Ballinger undid the hatch. It opened smoothly. Thankfully, Dick O'Kane had ordered his men to grease all such exits from the submarine in case they got jammed.[14]

Decker kept his nerve as Ballinger handed him the yellow wooden buoy attached to five hundred feet of line.

Decker pushed the buoy through the open hatch and released it. The line slithered out behind.

"Clay, count the knots as they go through your hand," said Ballinger.

Decker counted the knots on the line as they slipped through his hands: 100 feet, 110 feet, 150 feet . . .

The buoy soon reached the surface. Decker knew it because the line started to tug as the soccer-ball-like buoy was jostled by waves on the surface. The fathometer was correct. They were indeed 180 feet below the surface.

Decker now took the end of the line, reached out to the first rung of a ladder just outside the escape trunk, and tied the line off with three knots.

The four men stood together, nose to nose.

Decker attached his Momsen Lung's mouthpiece and then its nose clamp.

Ballinger nodded.

"OK, Clay—go for it."[15]

Decker ducked down into the water and exited the escape trunk, crawling out into utter blackness. The only way he could locate his hand was to touch his nose with it. All he knew was that he was standing on the outside of the hull. In the wooden deck above him was an opening around three feet wide. He had to reach it, had to find it. He clutched the line. If he didn't use it to guide him, he wouldn't know where to turn and could get lost finding the opening on the underside of the deck, become disoriented, panic, and drown.[16]

Decker held on to the line and followed it upward, through the blacked-out superstructure, through the opening in the deck, and then up into the cold ocean itself. He fought the urge to rise fast. Wrapping his legs and arms around the line, he looked up, but all he could see was darkness.

They were the longest seconds of his life. As each knot passed through his hands, he hesitated, inhaled, then exhaled as he moved up to the next knot. His careful ascent allowed him to equalize the internal pressure in his lungs with the external pressure. It kept him alive.[17]

Slowly, as Decker rose, the waters lightened. Finally, he could make out air bubbles shooting from his Momsen Lung to the surface far above. Somehow, he remained focused. Having gotten this far, only a hundred feet or so from life, he refused to give in to panic. He saw the water grow even lighter. Then he felt his head break the surface. There was daylight. He had made it.

Decker reached up to remove the nose clamp on his Momsen Lung. He felt blood. His nose and his cheeks were bleeding. But he had no sensation of pain or stinging. He realized that, although he had not come up fast enough to get the bends, he had risen a little faster than he should have, bursting superficial blood vessels on his face. In no time at all, however, the bleeding stopped, thanks to the salty, cold water.

Decker spat out the Momsen Lung's mouthpiece and then threw away the Lung. There were hand-holds on the yellow wooden buoy. He grabbed on to them. He could feel the pull of the current.[18]

A few moments later, Bill Ballinger surfaced a couple of yards away. He had clearly come up too fast. Decker watched in horror as he splashed frantically, bleeding, screaming, vomiting. His nose clamp was not on. He was just a few feet from Decker. Perhaps Ballinger's Momsen Lung discharge valve had been pinned shut like his own. No matter how carefully he may have risen, if he hadn't removed that pin, air wasn't releasing from his lungs, and they could have burst like a balloon as he neared the surface.[19]

Ballinger was clearly drowning. He was in agony.

A voice told Decker: "Don't touch that man! Don't you reach out and touch that man! Absolutely don't do it!"[20]

Ballinger caught sight of Decker. They looked at each other, "eyeball to eyeball."

Decker started to reach out to Ballinger but then stopped, terrified that he would be pulled down with him as Ballinger drowned.

That moment would stay with Decker forever. "Had he been able to get hold of me," he would recall decades later, "well, it's a known fact that a drowning man can pull a horse under the water. . . . I felt guilty. I could hear him screaming as he was [pulled away] by the tide, out to sea. But something had told me not to touch him."[21]

Decker had no way of knowing that four other survivors were already on the surface—the men who had been thrown from the bridge, like Bill Leibold, or who had jumped off, like Floyd Caverly. For all he knew, he was utterly alone. But, in fact, others were not too far from him, fighting to stay alive, men with nothing to hold onto but the hope of seeing loved ones again.

9

The Last Attempt

IN THE TORPEDO ROOM, it was now about five in the morning. Another forty minutes had passed with agonizing slowness.
Again there was no banging on the hull. Men put their ears to the
side of the trunk, listening for some signal, or anything at all. They
heard something. It sounded like a man moaning. Quickly, the ex-
terior door to the trunk was closed from the torpedo room and the
trunk drained. When they opened the hatch to the trunk, what
they saw shocked them to the core.

Hank Flanagan had collapsed and was unconscious, partially
wrapped in the escape line. Someone cut him free. Others carried
him down from the trunk, then placed him in a bunk and draped
a blanket over him. Another man was in the trunk, Basil Pearce,
the Floridian. He was in a stupor and had lost his nerve. After

recovering somewhat, he said he would not try again. But there was no reason, he added, perhaps trying to save face, why "every other man in the compartment shouldn't escape."[1]

Hope began to fade. The sight of the tough, wiry Flanagan being carried from the escape trunk, out cold, was terribly dispiriting. If Flanagan couldn't take the pressure, what chance did the others have, especially those who were injured and badly fatigued?

Others now decided that, like Pearce, they no longer had the strength to try to get out. More men took to bunks, pulling blankets over themselves, beginning to pray, their minds casting back over their lives, thinking especially of their families and wives.

Swish. Swish. Swish.

It was unmistakable, even to the most oxygen-starved of the men who were still conscious. It was the sound of a Japanese navy patrol boat's screws.[2] The Japanese had heard the men tapping on the bulkhead or banging about in the superstructure. Pete Narowanski was convinced of it.[3]

Try as they might, some of the men could not get others to be silent. It was as if some had given up hope and no longer cared if the Japanese detected them.[4]

The Japanese patrol boat finally passed over.

The end was near. Everyone knew it. They could hear it in the sound above. They could taste it in the poisoned air. And they could see it in smoke that was creeping into the forward torpedo room. The smoke came from the battery compartment and had found its way forward through the sinks in the officers' quarters, above the batteries.[5]

The men in the torpedo room managed to close some valves, but the toxic fumes kept seeping through. Someone tried to hammer wooden plugs into the drain to stop the fumes. But that didn't work either.

To combat yet another problem—the buildup of carbon dioxide—the men considered using an absorbent kept in every compartment of the submarine. "But [we] decided it was impracticable," one of them recalled, "as the large number of men in the compartment left no place to spread it out."[6]

Although the men had bled oxygen into the room several times, the level of oxygen in the air, normally eighteen to twenty-one percent, was now undoubtedly far below what was required to stay clear-headed. If it fell toward six percent, they would begin to lose consciousness and vomit. Below five percent, they would be seized by convulsions and begin gasping for air. Eventually, as the oxygen began to run out, they would lose dexterity and experience extreme fatigue, a sense of panic, and then profound lethargy before finally dying.

Then it began again. The Japanese started to drop depth charges once more. This time, apparently, the men stood or lay stock-still in silence, sweat streaming off their foreheads and chests.[7]

Finally, the explosions faded. A fire had broken out in the forward battery compartment.[8] Now its heat began to spread through the boat, sending the temperature soaring in the adjacent torpedo room.

The fire would steal more oxygen from their life-sustaining supply, which was already running out.

But it was the smoke from the fire that was of more immediate concern. It was going to asphyxiate anyone who stayed in the *Tang.* They all knew it. It was certain.[9]

Death could only be minutes away.

HAYES TRUKKE KNEW THE TIME had finally come. He had to get out and fast. It was now or never. No more officers were able or willing to take charge, so the Arizonan from Flagstaff mustered together a third escape party.[10]

Trukke climbed into the escape trunk with Pete Narowanski and two others. Narowanski looked as if he was going on vacation, dressed in brightly colored swimming trunks and a Hawaiian sports shirt. He had stuffed a can of Campbell's soup inside the belt of his trunks.[11]

Trukke looked around for the escape line. It had disappeared. They would have to float to the surface without a line. That would take enormous courage. It would also make it hard to find their way out of the superstructure.

Thinking quickly, Trukke climbed down into the forward torpedo room and picked up a Japanese life preserver that the crew had pulled out of the water after one of their successful attacks. He then climbed back into the escape trunk.[12] Narowanski saw the life preserver and recognized it as a souvenir from the *Yamaoka Maru,* which the *Tang* had destroyed on its third patrol.

The hatch below the men was sealed. Someone cranked an induction valve that let in sea water.[13] The trunk began to flood once more. Trukke placed his Momsen Lung close to the oxygen outlet in the trunk to charge it. It didn't work. The supply was empty. It needed to be restored by turning on a valve in the torpedo room below. But there was no way of communicating this to the men there and invaluable time would be wasted if they had to drain the trunk, open the hatch, and repeat the process all over again.

Trukke then remembered his survival training at submarine school. He knew it was possible to rise to the surface without breathing apparatus. There was no need to panic. He told the three men with him that they could still ascend, even from 180 feet below. The method had never been tried before from a submerged American submarine, but it was possible. By steadily exhaling air as they rose to the surface, Trukke explained, they could equalize the pressure in their lungs with that of the water and avoid the bends.

The three other men squashed into the escape trunk were understandably not so sure. They still wanted to fill their Momsen Lungs with oxygen. Suddenly, Narowanski's closest friend on the *Tang,* Torpedoman John Fluker, began to scream with pain.

Narowanksi tried to soothe him. There were just a few more pounds of pressure to endure, he said, before it would be equalized with the sea outside, and then the external door could be opened. But Fluker was close to unconsciousness because of the pressure.

Then there was yet another, potentially fatal hitch—they couldn't open the external door. Frantically, they hammered away at it. Finally, it gave. Had the pressure inside the trunk not risen sufficiently to allow the door to open with ease?

Water surged in and then, after a few agonizing moments, settled back until it reached their chests. Testing their Momsen Lungs, they made a crucial, heartening discovery—they didn't need to fill the Momsen Lungs with oxygen after all. Their own breath would suffice to fill the lung.

Hayes Trukke knew he had only a few seconds left. He was fading fast: "I felt very exhausted—like I couldn't get any oxygen into my lungs and began to get dizzy, so I knew I had better get out while I could."[14] Grabbing the life preserver, he pulled himself out of the trunk into the superstructure, where he discovered the escape line leading to the buoy on the surface. Fortunately, Clay Decker had tied it to a rung in the ladder connected to the decking above. Trukke hadn't needed the life preserver after all. But he held onto it anyway, following the escape line through the superstructure to the three-foot-wide opening to the wooden deck. He was still wearing his Momsen Lung, knowing it would help him float on the surface.

Trukke climbed out of the *Tang* and followed the line upward. Because he was holding on to the life preserver, which provided extra flotation, he began to rise too fast. Below him, Pete Narowanski felt the line jerking and pulled on it, hoping to indicate to Trukke that he should slow his ascent. But instead he tugged Trukke's Momsen Lung free from him. Trukke was only 20 feet above the *Tang*, as much as 160 feet from the surface, when it broke loose and drifted away.[15]

He didn't panic. He just carried on as slowly as possible, breathing out steadily so he could avoid the bends. The water finally began to lighten. Then his head was above the slightly choppy surface. He wasn't coughing up blood. He could breathe. He could taste saltwater. It was bright daylight. But then he vomited and it seemed like he couldn't stop. He was close to passing out but somehow found the strength to stay afloat until he could grab the life preserver.

After a few minutes, Trukke heard a voice. It belonged to Clay Decker. He looked around and saw him, fifty yards away. Trukke struck out, got to Decker, and then clung to the yellow buoy.[16] Together they attached the life preserver to the buoy.

As the two survivors held on, treading water, they decided to get rid of any extra weight. They let go of their guns and C-rations, anything that could pull them down. They knew instinctively that they would need all the strength they could muster to stay afloat, to stay alive.[17]

BACK IN THE ESCAPE TRUNK, John Fluker could take it no more. He and the remaining men decided to abort the attempt.[18] The door was closed and then Pete Narowanksi banged on the trunk, giving the signal to the men below to drain the trunk. Would the Japanese also hear his signal? Time would tell.

The hatch was opened from below. Fluker somehow had enough strength left to climb down from the trunk into the torpedo room. Badly shaken, he said he didn't want to try again. The experience had been too much.

Meanwhile, Narowanski stayed put in the trunk. He was now determined to live. He wasn't the kind to lose heart and go lie in a bunk and die. On the waterfront in Depression-era Baltimore, he had stolen bags of potatoes off merchant ships to help feed his nine siblings.[19] After leaving school in the eighth grade, he had worked in a tin mill, carousing and playing the horses. He had later married a sixteen-year-old girl after getting her pregnant with his now four-year-old daughter, Jackie. Marriage hadn't suited him and he quickly divorced, preferring to run with his pals and gamble on the horses and hunt deer—perhaps his greatest passion—than to stay home with his young wife.[20] Now if he died trying, so be it, but Pete Narowanksi wasn't ready to give up on his young child, his beloved mother, Anya, and his fast horses, not just yet.

Narowanski called down into the torpedo room. He wanted someone to open the last oxygen valve so he and others could charge their Momsen Lungs from inside the trunk.[21]

In the meantime, Lieutenant Hank Flanagan had regained consciousness. He decided to join Narowanski in the escape trunk. There was no time to lose: Flanagan could see smoke seeping through the rubber seals in the hatch leading from the forward torpedo room to the next compartment. Soon, the seals would break and dense smoke and chlorine gas would fill the torpedo room, quickly killing all those still alive.

Flanagan could also see paint beginning to blister on the bulkhead near him, so intense was the heat in the torpedo room. The fire in the adjacent compartment was growing fiercer. There was no doubt about it. If Flanagan didn't get out in the next escape party, the *Tang* would become his "iron coffin."[22]

Flanagan climbed into the escape trunk once more.

Not far away, Jesse DaSilva stood near the torpedo tubes, several feet from the ladder leading to the escape trunk. In the increasing gloom, he could see some men gathering beneath the trunk.

"We need someone else," yelled Flanagan.

DaSilva turned to a close friend, Motor Mechanic Glen Haws. DaSilva knew that Haws's wife, Myhrl, was pregnant, due to give birth any day.[23] DaSilva told Haws to go before him and climb into the trunk. Haws had a wife. A family to care for. DaSilva didn't.[24]

Flanagan called down again from the escape trunk. He was losing patience. He told DaSilva and Haws to get going. They were running out of time.

Haws hesitated.[25]

"Hell, I'm not afraid to try," said DaSilva, who then climbed up the ladder to the escape trunk.[26]

But DaSilva apparently couldn't turn his back on his close friend. He made one last attempt to persuade Haws.

"Come on!" he implored.[27]

Haws was still not willing to try.

Someone else took his place.

The time was eight o'clock. Almost six hours had passed since the *Tang* had sunk herself. DaSilva knew it because he looked at a clock on the bulkhead.

Most of the survivors of the initial blast were now lying down in bunks, praying or talking in hushed voices about their families. Several had already passed out.[28] Those who were still conscious coughed and choked, or tried using their Momsen Lungs.

There was no panic. The injured men who knew they couldn't make the escape seemed to have quietly resigned themselves to death. DaSilva figured that others had already convinced themselves that "they would likely foul things up for someone else if they tried. They were content with the fact that that was it. They were just laying there in the bunk, waiting to die."[29]

It was possible that some of the men laying silently in the bunks were already dead, their bodies having finally succumbed to the deadly combination of poisonous fumes from the battery fire, ever increasing levels of carbon dioxide, and the intense heat, which caused extreme dehydration.

Doc Larson tended as best he could to those he could still help. He may have decided to stay with the wounded as long as possible and only leave with the very last party. There was still some oxygen left in the forward torpedo room, which meant there was still perhaps time for another escape attempt after Narowanski's party. Larson might still make it.

In the escape trunk, Narowanski took charge. The hatch was sealed from below. Then Narowanksi began to flood the trunk. As the water rose, the men felt stabbing pains in their ears. They held their noses and blew out, trying to equalize the pressure. "We started flooding the compartment and, boy, when you flood that thing," recalled DaSilva, "the air really gets tough. I mean, it gets hard to breathe. At 180 feet, your pressure is really great."[30]

The men felt as if they were going to suffocate. DaSilva saw the water rise above the side door. Finally, it was up to their chests. Their voices were now so high-pitched they were almost inaudible.[31] Their hearts racing, they tested their Momsen Lungs, ducking their heads below the water. Then someone opened the door to the superstructure. Narowanski grabbed on to the escape line and exited. He was followed by Hank Flanagan and then by DaSilva. The last man was supposed to follow and close the door behind him.

DaSilva felt his way through the superstructure and then climbed through the hatch leading to the ocean. Immediately, the water pressure grabbed at him, forcing his body upward. He resisted the urge to let go of the line and surge to the surface.[32] "I wrapped my feet around the rope," he remembered, "and slowly let myself up ten feet at a time, stopping to count to ten each time."

DaSilva was about a hundred feet from the surface, in pitch darkness, when he started to have problems breathing. He slowed his ascent.[33]

How slow should I go? thought DaSilva. *Gotta stop every ten feet . . . or was it fifteen feet?*

Is the other man coming up in back of me?

Tighten your grip with your feet, or you will turn upside down.

Where the hell is that next knot?

The waters were black and cold.

Did I stop at that last knot?

How long have I been coming up?

He was rising too fast.

Slow down and breathe deep.

It was still dark. He was still far from the surface.

Should be seeing light by now.

Who's already up there?

Still the frigid darkness.

Where the hell is the surface?

Wish there was a rescue team waiting.

Maybe the Japs are there.

He found a knot.

STOP! Now slow . . . Up . . . Up . . . Up . . .[34]

DaSilva realized he was able to breathe easier. The air in his lungs was equalizing with the external pressure.

No more darkness. When he exhaled, he could see bubbles escape from his Momsen Lung and then shoot upward, like the fizz in a glass of champagne.

DaSilva finally broke the surface. He was not puking. He felt tired but was fully conscious. "Hell, I felt fine," he recalled. "I didn't have any aftereffects or anything."[35]

DaSilva saw the bow of a ship the *Tang* had sunk the night before and, far in the distance, the coast of mainland China. Then he spotted Hank Flanagan and Pete Narowanski. They were nearby. They too had made it and looked in reasonable condition. DaSilva then caught sight of Hayes Trukke and Clayton Decker holding onto the soccer-sized buoy. They were treading water.

Pete Narowanski could see the moon setting in the early morning sky. As he swam toward the buoy, he thought of his four-year-old daughter, Jackie, with her dark complexion and long, auburn pigtails. She was being brought up by his parents in the country, near Turners Station in Maryland. Thinking about her and about his mother, who had doted on him and now on Jackie, gave him added strength.[36]

Soon, all five of the men were clinging to the buoy, looking at the coast of China. It did not seem too far away. But the current was pulling in the opposite direction. Decker knew he could not possibly swim so far, at least ten miles, against the current in his condition. But Pete Narowanski and Hayes Trukke decided to risk it and struck out for the coast. After only a minute or so, they realized they would never manage to get there, so swift was the opposing current, and they headed back to the buoy.

AT 180 FEET BELOW, a last group was gathering at the steps to the escape trunk. It included Doc Larson, the husky six-foot-tall Iowan, and the steward, Howard Walker—O'Kane's favorite "chronic gambler." It is not known who else was with them, if indeed there were any others. Conditions in the forward torpedo room were probably intolerable without the aid of a Momsen Lung. More and more toxic smoke had seeped in, gradually asphyxiating men who were still conscious. There was precious little oxygen and the heat was just as suffocating as the poisoned air.

Somehow, Larson and the badly injured Walker were able to flood the escape trunk, endure the earsplitting increase in pressure as the water rose, and open the door. What happened next will never be known. But it is likely that both Walker's and Larson's senses were so dulled that they made terrible errors as they struggled to get out of the *Tang* and then to the surface.

Larson appeared first, not far from the men gathered around the buoy, which suggested he had followed the line up. He was in a shocking state, barely alive, stricken by the bends and a probable lung embolism. Perhaps he had failed to exhale as he rose. Or maybe his Momsen Lung had malfunctioned. In his rush to get out of the escape trunk, he could have forgotten to test the equipment. In any case, his lungs and eardrums were severely damaged. Blood was running out of his ears, his nose, and his mouth. He could hardly breathe.[37]

The captain. Richard O'Kane at Annapolis
before his graduation in 1934.
(*Courtesy O'Kane family*)

The O'Kanes. Rear Admiral W. L. Friedell, Commandant
Mare Island Navy Yard, welcomes Lt. Commander Richard O'Kane,
Executive Officer, USS *Wahoo*, and his family back to
Mare Island for a re-fit in May 1943. (*U.S. Navy*)

George Zofcin in
wartime San Francisco.
(*Courtesy Zofcin family*)

Jesse DaSilva at submarine
training school in San Diego.
(*Courtesy DaSilva family*)

Floyd Caverly before leaving Pearl
Harbor on the *Tang*'s final patrol.
(*Courtesy Caverly family*)

"Uncle Charlie,"
Vice Admiral Charles Lockwood,
Commander Submarines Pacific.
(*U.S. Navy*)

Bill "Boats" Leibold.
(*Courtesy Leibold family*)

The U.S.S. *Tang* in Pearl Harbor, 1944. (*U.S. Navy*)

The tower used for escape training at submarine school in New London, Connecticut. (*U.S. Navy*)

Escape training using the Momsen Lung at submarine school. (*U.S. Navy*)

Richard O'Kane, left, with his mentor, Dudley "Mush" Morton, 1943. (*U.S. Navy*)

Richard O'Kane with twenty-two rescued airmen. (*U.S. Navy*)

The submarine dock at Midway. (*U.S. Navy*)

The *Tang*'s battle flag. (*Courtesy Leibold and DaSilva families*)

The U.S.S. *Tang*. (*Courtesy DaSilva family*)

The docks at Mare Island. (*U.S. Navy*)

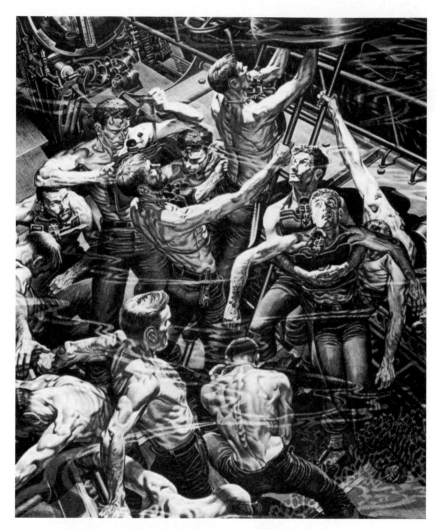

An artist's depiction of men trying to escape the *Tang*.
(*Original painting by Fred Freeman for U.S. Navy*)

OPPOSITE:
Omori, built on a man-made island, in Tokyo Bay.
(*Courtesy Da Silva family*)

Emaciated
POWs in Omori,
1945. (*Courtesy
DaSilva family*)

RIGHT:
POW camp as it
looked to American
pilots dropping
supplies, August
1945. (*Courtesy
Da Silva family*)

Japanese guards bowing to liberated POWs in Ofuna,
the "Torture Farm." (*National Archives*)

Major Greg "Pappy" Boyington
shaking hands with a liberator.
(*Courtesy DaSilva family*)

Freedom. Clay Decker, third on left from man holding Stars and Stripes, and fellow prisoners celebrate liberation on August 29,1945. (*U.S. Navy*)

Men in Omori rejoice upon liberation. Note Jesse DaSilva at bottom right and Floyd Caverly in center. (*Courtesy DaSilva family*)

The Japanese formal surrender in Tokyo Bay. (*National Archives*)

Newspaper photograph of
Grace Leibold, seconds after
being told by a reporter that
her husband was alive.
(*Courtesy Leibold family*)

Newspaper photograph of Floyd
Caverly and his wife, Leone, and
daughter Mary Anne enjoying their first
Christmas together, December 1945.
(*Courtesy Caverly family*)

Pete Narowanski and his daughter Jackie
after the war. (*Courtesy Narowanski family*)

"The Bravest Man." President Truman shakes O'Kane's hand after presenting him with the Medal of Honor, on the White House lawn, March 1946. (*National Archives*)

Three of the nine. Newspaper photograph of Bill Leibold, Floyd Caverly, and Richard O'Kane at a press conference in San Francisco in 1947. (*San Francisco Examiner*)

Happy campers. The O'Kane family in Kings Canyon, Sequoia National Park, 1947. The trailer, designed by Richard O'Kane, was built to be "as compact as a submarine inside," according to Marsha O'Kane, seated opposite her brother, Jim, and mother, Ernestine. (*Courtesy O'Kane family*)

Sailor on horseback. Richard O'Kane at his ranch in northern
California in the early 1980s. (*Courtesy O'Kane family*)

Jesse DaSilva with Ernestine O'Kane at
submarine veteran's reunion. (*Courtesy DaSilva family*)

Reunited. The survivors at a *Tang* reunion in 1988.
(*Courtesy DaSilva family*)

Survivors and their wives at Decker's house in Denver, 1991:
from left to right, Grace and Bill Leibold, Ann and Clay Decker,
Floyd and Betty Caverly, Ernestine and Dick O'Kane,
Joyce and Jesse DaSilva. (*Courtesy DaSilva family*)

Narowanski and DaSilva swam to Larson's side and pulled him over to the buoy. Larson could not even manage to keep his head above the surface. DaSilva tried to get Larson to hold onto the buoy but it was useless. The soft-spoken Iowan, a favorite with all the men aboard, was clearly dying. As he drifted in and out of consciousness, his last thoughts may have been about his family and wife, Caryl, who worked in a beauty parlor in Harlan, Iowa.

Then another man's head appeared above the surface, between twenty to fifty feet away. It was Howard Walker. That he was farther away than Larson had been on surfacing suggested that he had let go of the line at some point during his ascent. He was not wearing a Momsen Lung. His badly injured nose may have prevented him from using it. Walker was flailing around in the water as if he couldn't swim.

Jesse DaSilva still had plenty of energy. He struck out toward Walker but Walker suddenly went under, disappearing before DaSilva could reach him. One of the other men saw Walker's body drift away. His head was under the water but visible for a while.[38] "The tide was going out to sea, and before you know it, well he just disappeared," recalled DaSilva. "I turned around and it took me forever to get back to the guys because the tide was going out."[39]

The men turned their attention to Larson, trying to keep him alive. "We managed to hold on to him [and] keep him afloat," recalled Decker. "He was not fighting us or anything like that. He had taken water in his lungs. Had we been on the beach, we might have been able to save him."[40]

The sun rose in the sky. It was sometime after nine o'clock. The men were exhausted, parched, and beginning to lose their last reserves of strength. But they had done what no other American had managed before. They had won an important victory over the ocean—they had escaped from a submerged submarine without help from the surface. Of the more than 3,500 Americans lost in sunken submarines during the war, they alone had survived. They had made history.[41]

A FEW MILES AWAY, Japanese sailors aboard a patrol boat, the *P-34*, dropped a buoy into the ocean. Then the *P-34* began to sweep in a circle. Throughout the night, its crew had been searching for survivors from the ships sunk by the *Tang*.[42] Some of the bedraggled men fished from the oil-slicked waters now lay in a desperate state on the deck or sat huddled under blankets. Several were in terrible pain from steam burns caused by exploding boilers.

A lifeboat was lowered from the *P-34*'s main deck. Two sailors armed with rifles sat in the boat and began rowing toward the exposed bow of one of the ships that the *Tang* had sunk the night before.

The Japanese sailors spotted Leibold and Caverly, who had now been treading water for almost eight hours.

Leibold and Caverly could not yet see the lifeboat, but they could see the bow of the last ship they had sunk the night before.

"Let's get over to that ship," said Leibold. "If we can get on there maybe we can get ahold of a lifeboat or something like that and we can get to the coast of China."[43]

Leibold and Caverly were about to swim over when they finally saw the two Japanese sailors in the *P-34*'s lifeboat. It was about 9:30 in the morning.

Caverly and Leibold called out to them, but the Japanese could not understand a word they said.[44]

The Japanese were clearly puzzled by their Caucasian faces.

One of the Japanese sailors, who looked to be the boat's coxswain, began talking to them.

"Doitsu ka?" asked the Japanese (meaning "Are you German?").

The Japanese hauled Caverly and Leibold aboard.

Caverly slapped one of the Japanese on the back as a way of thanking him for pulling him out of the water.[45] The Japanese sailor was not amused and growled at Caverly.

The coxswain kept repeating "Doitsu ka?," thinking he had picked up two German sailors who had been on one of the Japanese ships, not realizing that they were American submariners responsible for the destruction wreaked the night before.

"They think we're krauts," Caverly told Leibold.

Caverly turned to the coxswain and then said. "Heil Hitler!"[46]

The Japanese began to row back toward the P-34. Soon they caught sight of a head bobbing in the water. As they neared, they could see a man lying on a wooden door. The boat drew closer. It was Dick O'Kane.[47]

Leibold and Caverly leaned over and began to haul O'Kane aboard. "Good morning, Captain. Do you want a ride?" said Leibold.

The coxswain overheard the word "captain" and now realized he had picked up American sailors and their captain. He motioned for O'Kane to sit in the stern, the assigned place for officers. With its passengers under guard, the lifeboat returned to the P-34, where it was hoisted up to the main deck.[48]

As Caverly stepped out of the boat and onto the deck, he noticed a deckhand's wristwatch. Leaning over, he grabbed the man's wrist to check the time. It was 10:30 a.m. The deckhand punched

Caverly in the face. As Caverly later recalled, he had received his "first knuckle sandwich" from the Japanese. There would be plenty more.[49]

LARRY SAVADKIN HAD NOW been floating for over eight hours. Every quarter of an hour, he had refilled his makeshift life preserver—his inflated pants. Several times during the night, the Japanese had dropped depth charges, and he had felt the shock waves from each explosion. At one point, he had struck out to the west but had then realized quickly that the current was too strong to make progress, and in any case he could not orientate himself by the stars.[50]

Savadkin could see the faint outline of the coast of China. He could also make out several Japanese ships in the far distance, one of them the *P-34*. He guessed they were combing the area looking for survivors from the previous night's battle.

At first, Savadkin tried to not be spotted by the Japanese ships, but then he realized that he would eventually drown because he was starting to suffer from hypothermia. So he yelled and splashed the water. It worked. He was soon spotted by the *P-34*'s lifeboat, hauled aboard, and then taken to the *P-34*.[51]

The lifeboat then returned to the area to search for more survivors.

MEANWHILE, THE FIVE MEN who had escaped from the submerged *Tang* still clung to the yellow buoy and each other. They could see the *Tang*'s last victim around five hundred yards away, its bow sticking up above the surface. They agreed to wait until there was a favorable current, and then swim to the bow and find a life raft or some other object on which they could float to China.

Then the Japanese lifeboat came into sight. It approached slowly. One of the Japanese sailors aimed his gun at the *Tang* survivors.

Well, this is it, thought DaSilva. *They're going to shoot us.*[52]

To DaSilva's surprise, the Japanese held his fire.[53] He indicated that the men were to board at the aft end of the lifeboat while they stayed at the bow. Before climbing aboard themselves, the men helped Larson into the boat. One of the Japanese sailors tried to bring him around by slapping him. But it was no use. He had stopped breathing.[54]

The other Japanese sailor then attempted to pull the buoy, with the Japanese life preserver attached to it, out of the water. "We didn't dare tell him it was anchored to a submarine down there," recalled Decker.[55] The sailor kept yanking on the buoy but still could not pull it aboard. Finally, he cursed and gave up.

The two Japanese sailors rowed the five *Tang* survivors to the P-34. A rope ladder was lowered from the ship, and one by one the men ascended. Clay Decker was the last man to climb up. He later claimed that as he neared the deck, he looked over his shoulder and saw the two Japanese sailors dumping Larson's body over the side of the lifeboat.[56]

THERE WERE NOW NINE MEN who were still alive. According to the commander of the Pacific's submarine fleet, Vice Admiral Charles Lockwood, they had participated in the "greatest submarine cruise of all time."[57] Some had journeyed more than twice around the earth in total distance with the *Tang*, sinking a ship on average every eleven days. But seventy-eight of their friends had now been lost, proving in O'Kane's words that "in war there can be an inverse moral: the greater the performance, the harsher the consequence."[58]

Without doubt, more of their comrades would have found the strength and courage to escape the deep had they not been so afraid of ending up in exactly the situation that the *Tang* survivors now found themselves in. Before long, some of those still alive would begin to wonder whether they too would have been better off staying down with the *Tang*, being slowly lulled into unconsciousness and finally drifting off into death. At least they would not be at the mercy of the sadistic and vengeful Japanese; their nightmare would be over. Instead, a new battle for survival was about to begin.

PART THREE

Captivity

Prisoners of war are in the power of the hostile Power,
but not of the individuals or corps who have captured them.
They must at all times be humanely treated and protected,
particularly against acts of violence, insults and public curiosity.
Measures of reprisal against them are prohibited.

—The 1929 Geneva Convention Relative to
the Treatment of Prisoners of War

10

Guests of
the Japanese

NINE MEN HAD SURVIVED—nine of eighty-seven. Their
fate was now in Japanese hands. Like most Americans,
they had been indoctrinated to view the "Japs" as an inferior race.
Stories of Japanese atrocities, of staggering brutality, were legion
by this point in the war. It was therefore all the more distressing
and humiliating to be taken prisoner by them. "There was a lot of
worry," recalled Floyd Caverly. "You didn't know what to expect
from them."[1]

Caverly spotted dozens of Japanese sailors lying on the deck,
many of them with severe burns and other injuries—survivors

from the previous night's onslaught. How long before they realized that the Americans fished from the water were responsible for
their injuries and the deaths of so many of their comrades?
Caverly calculated that the *Tang* had sunk five ships the previous
night—more than enough to justify savage revenge.[2]

The Japanese promptly tied up the survivors. Their arms were
pinned to their chests and their wrists were bound together. Then
they were made to sit down on the port side of the main deck.[3]
Badly injured Japanese were just a few yards away. They, also, had
just been rescued.

Bill Leibold looked at the horribly burned Japanese survivors
and became concerned.[4] "To put it mildly, we were all apprehen-
sive," he recalled. "There were a lot of [them] who had apparently
been burned and otherwise banged up, and they didn't look on us
too kindly."[5]

The *P-34* patrol boat kept looking for survivors. No more were
found from the *Tang*, but some Japanese were fished from the waters. Meanwhile, the Americans sat on the forecastle's decking beneath the blazing sun. "It was the roughest time we had, sitting
on the hot steel deck of that ship," recalled Clay Decker. "When
we went aboard we were in our shorts and a shirt, and that was it.
A submariner doesn't get any sunshine. Our skin was really fair.
We were soon very sunburned. Our lips were blistered and
swollen."[6]

The survivors felt as if they were sitting in a frying pan. Yet they
could not move or shift their weight around to ease their pain.

The sun's rays felt more intense as the hours passed. Throughout the day, the men were not given food or water. "It kept getting
hotter and we kept asking for water," recalled Bill Leibold. "Finally
they brought us water . . . but it was boiling."

Their suffering had only just begun. The *Tang* crew were about to find out that the Japanese harbored enormous contempt for enemy submarine crews, who had caused immense damage to their war effort.

At first, some of the Japanese survivors began to circle the *Tang* men, then they started kicking and slapping them. "Hog-tied like we were," recalled Savadkin, "we just had to take it."[7]

The sailors grabbed the *Tang* survivors by the hair, yanked back their heads, and stubbed out cigarettes on their faces and necks. The sailors had plenty to be angry about. In the *Tang's* attack on their ship, "a steam boiler had busted open and some of the [Japanese] survivors were scalded like lobsters," recalled Decker. "Soon enough, they realized, 'Hey, here's the guys who did this to us.' They grabbed me by the hair, took a lit cigarette, and stuck it up my nose. They hit us with rifle butts and kicked us."[8]

Floyd Caverly was kneeling with his hands and feet tied together.

A Japanese officer approached.

"What is the name of your ship?" asked the officer in English.

Caverly had been told never to divulge information to the enemy.

"What is the name of your boat?"[9]

"We didn't have a boat name," lied Caverly. "Just a number."

The officer pulled out his sword.

"What was the name of your boat?"

"There was no name, sir."

Caverly prepared to die.

The officer lifted his sword. Then he swiped Caverly with it. But he didn't kill him. Instead he hit him alongside the head with the flat side of the sword.

Caverly didn't feel too much pain. "I thought I'd have to go over the side of the boat after my head if I wanted one," he recalled. "I figured that was the end."[10]

Caverly was sitting between O'Kane, to his left, and Torpedoman Hayes Trukke, to his right.

"Who is that next to you?" asked O'Kane.

"Trukke," said Caverly.

O'Kane seemed surprised.

"Was he on board my boat?"

Caverly nodded.

Trukke had joined the *Tang* just before her final patrol. After being in the water, his wet hair now hung over his face.

Caverly looked at Trukke. He reminded him of a popular cartoon character who had long blonde hair. "O'Kane was a stickler for short haircuts and no beards," recalled Caverly. "He was amazed, I guess, that someone was on his submarine who had long, scraggly hair."[11]

IT DIDN'T TAKE LONG for the Japanese to realize that the *Tang* survivors were submariners and—more ominously—that they had rescued the very men who had caused such heavy damage and loss of life to their convoy in previous days. It seemed hard to credit, at first, that these few, bedraggled Americans had been responsible for the holocaust the evening before.

One by one, the *Tang* survivors were taken belowdecks to be questioned. "When it was my turn," recalled Jesse DaSilva, "they took me to another part of the ship and had me sit down between three of them. They offered me a ball of rice, but I could not eat it. One of them had an electrical device and he would jab me in the ribs with this and I would twitch and jump. They all thought this was very funny. The one that could speak English carried a large club about the size of a baseball bat. He would ask questions and if he didn't like the answers he would hit me on the head with this bat. After some time, when they figured that I wasn't going to tell them anything, they took me back to the others."[12]

When the sun began to set on their first day in captivity, the *Tang* survivors were crammed together into a small deckhouse. There was only enough space for them to stand. Out of earshot of the Japanese, they talked about their escape from the *Tang*.

The deckhouse soon felt like a sauna, more uncomfortable even than the frying-pan deck. "It was extremely hot in there," recalled Leibold. "It was all metal. There was a wooden door with an opening at the bottom and the top. The opening was about six inches at the top. A guard stood outside. When we asked for water and food, the guard thrust his bayonet through the opening."[13]

The next morning, the Japanese again began to question the survivors.

Bill Leibold was taken belowdecks and interrogated. He refused to provide any information beyond his name, rating, and service number, as stipulated by the Geneva convention. But the Japanese insisted on more information.

"What was the name of your submarine?"

When Leibold refused to answer, he was beaten.

Leibold was not the only survivor who was hit for not revealing the name of the *Tang*. Others were soon nursing serious bruises. Their captain, Dick O'Kane, realized that there was little to be gained by refusing to reveal the *Tang*'s identity. His men were already suffering enough; they were extremely dehydrated and exhausted, surviving on adrenaline and little else. The violence had to stop or someone would die.

"Listen," O'Kane told his men, "The *Tang*'s on the bottom. Just go ahead and tell them what the name is."[14]

THE AGONY SEEMED as if it would never end. For four more days, the *Tang* survivors fried in the daytime sun on the *P-34*'s deck and were crammed together in the airless deckhouse at night. Some of the men recalled with bitter irony how they had treated a Japanese sailor from Kyoto, a man named Mishuitunni Ka, whom they had fished from the water on their third patrol. They had nicknamed the sailor "Firecracker" because they had saved his life on July 4, 1944.

In stark contrast to what they were experiencing, the *Tang*'s crew had looked after Firecracker so well that O'Kane noted he was "much more of a crew's mascot than a prisoner of war." In fact, he was treated more like a guest of honor: One midnight, while passing through the galley, O'Kane had found a cook hard at work. "Oh, I'm just trying to get the texture of Firecracker's rice the way he's used to it, Captain," the cook had commented. "We've been cooking it too hard."[15]

On the fifth day aboard the *P-34*, the men were sitting on the deck when they saw the Pescadores Islands come into view. Then the *P-34* entered the port of Takao on Formosa, modern-day Taiwan.

As they entered the harbor, the *Tang*'s survivors were blind-folded. "They [also] put a hangman's black sack over our heads," recalled Larry Savadkin.[16]

After the Japanese led the men off the boat, they were bundled
onto a flatbed truck, which took them to a dockside warehouse.
"The Japanese then waltzed us through a small town," recalled Bill
Leibold, describing the public procession the men next endured.
"There was a lot of yelling. We got pushed around."[17]

O'Kane later observed that this "morning publicity parade
rather backfired. Trukke had somehow managed to keep long
blonde hair, but now all of the slickum had washed away, and his
hair bounded down all around to the level of his mouth, giving
him the exact appearance of Hairless Joe in Al Capp's comic strip.
The onlookers pointed and laughed [at him] until the whole affair
took on—for them—the nature of a circus parade."[18]

After the march, the *Tang* survivors were placed in a jail. A Japanese
officer threatened them with beheading if they did not cooperate.
In their cells, the *Tang* survivors were chained by the
wrists to rings fixed high on the wall. Unable to swat away clouds
of bugs that soon descended, they were quickly covered with terrible
bites from mosquitoes.

Through much of the night, the Japanese interrogated the
Tang's survivors.[19] "Several times two or three Japanese would
come and shine a flashlight in my face and start asking me some
questions," remembered Jesse DaSilva. "When they did not get
the answers they would like, they would slap me across the face.
When morning came, they lined us all up again."

The men were given old white Japanese navy uniforms, put on
a truck, taken to a station, and then loaded on a train for an all-
day journey up the coast. Their blindfolds were removed once they
were on the train. They saw that each of them was guarded. It was
a regular passenger car. The shades were drawn until they left the
station.

Jesse DaSilva stared through the window. He felt as if he were looking back a hundred years. Peasants toiled in the fields with hand plows pulled by oxen. There was no sign of mechanization.

Finally, the men arrived at the other end of Formosa in the port city of Kiirun.[20] It was raining and dark when they were taken off the train and placed on a truck that took them a few miles from the city. "The truck stopped in front of some building and they marched us in there," recalled Jesse DaSilva. "Blindfolded, we stood before some officials until the blindfolds were removed. There were a few words said, then the blindfolds were put back on and we were taken back to the truck and taken to some old buildings."

The buildings were an old, stone Portuguese prison, which the men nicknamed "Kiirun Clink." They were then separated from each other and taken to cells with dirt and gravel floors. "The cells were set above the guards' catwalk like the cages in a zoo," recalled Larry Savadkin. "The bars were of wood, but about five inches in diameter stretching from the ceiling to the floor. The [toilet] was a hole in the floor set back in a niche."[21]

To the men's surprise, they were provided with blankets and then served a meal—balls of rice and fish wrapped in leaves. It was their first real nourishment in almost a week, since the October 25 sinking. "They also brought us some hot tea," recalled Leibold. "We slept. They didn't fool with us at all."[22]

The Kiirun Clink guards were not all brutes. In fact one, who had been conscripted, was memorably humane. "He crept into my cell," recalled Larry Savadkin, "and in broken English told me he was a Christian, and he had a present for the boys."

The guard gave his "present" to Savadkin and then slipped away.

The other men in their cells were asleep.

Savadkin held the presents behind his back.

"Hey!" he said, waking some of the men. "Guess what I've got for you—ice cream on a stick!"

"Take it easy, Mr. Savadkin," replied one of the men.

The men looked in amazement as Savadkin revealed the guard's gifts. "They thought I was completely off my rocker," he recalled. "But sure enough, that was what the guard had produced: one long, cool, drippy, and wonderfully sticky Popsicle on a stick for each of us. It was a great day."[23]

THE *Tang* survivors were soon on the move again. This time they were loaded onto a bizarre-looking, charcoal-fired bus—evidence of the Japanese's vastly diminished fuel supplies thanks to the devastating effect of American submarine warfare. "It had a little boiler on the tail end of it," recalled Bill Leibold. "Each of us was assigned a guard who carried a rifle. After a while, the bus stopped and the guards got out and started pushing the bus. They left their rifles on the bus."[24]

The men knew there was no point trying to escape—they would simply be rounded up and probably killed.

The bus finally stopped in a harbor where the officers were separated from the noncommissioned men. The officers—Savadkin, O'Kane, and Flanagan—were taken to a destroyer for transport to mainland Japan, while the enlisted men—Caverly, DaSilva, Decker, Narowanski, Leibold, and Trukke—went to a cruiser where they were placed in a hold full of sacks of sugar cane. Every now and again, Japanese sailors would enter, punch holes in the sacks, and fill up little bags of sugar.²⁵ The survivors realized that the U.S. blockade of Japan must have become so severe that sugar was as rare as gold.

On board the destroyer, Dick O'Kane was treated with unusual respect during his journey to mainland Japan. O'Kane had even been greeted by the customary ceremonial formation of sideboys as he boarded the destroyer. He was then escorted by its captain to a large stateroom. The Japanese captain told O'Kane he would return to talk to him from time to time. An armed guard stood in front of the open door—the sole reminder, it seemed, that this was not, after all, a pleasure cruise.

O'Kane looked through the open door and watched the crew performing their drills and duties. It was depressing to see an enemy gun crew going through a drill with impressive discipline. He was then given shoes and clothes, and fed properly. It was after dark when the Japanese captain, who was about O'Kane's age, returned to the cabin to talk to him. At first they discussed tactics. The Japanese captain said it was unlikely now that there would be a large-scale, decisive sea battle between what was left of the Japanese navy and the Americans.

"How is it, commander, that you speak no Japanese but seem to understand my English?" asked the Japanese captain.

O'Kane said Japanese was not offered as a course when he had been at Annapolis.

The Japanese captain looked at O'Kane.

"How could we expect to understand each other's problems when you made no attempt to learn even a word of our language?"

The Japanese captain returned to his duties. O'Kane's thoughts turned to the last torpedo he had fired. *How had a circular run been possible?* Torpedoes on his previous surface ships had been fitted with safety mechanisms to prevent circular runs.

If only the *Tang* had had the same.

FINALLY, THE *Tang* survivors neared mainland Japan. Aboard the destroyer, O'Kane returned his clean clothing and comfortable shoes, having been told he would get a new uniform when he got ashore. He thanked the Japanese captain as he left the boat.

Why, asked O'Kane, had he been treated so well on the destroyer but not on the *P-34* patrol boat?

"That ship and the escort force," said the Japanese captain, "are not part of the Imperial Japanese Navy."[26]

O'Kane went down the gangway and stepped onto Japanese soil in Kobe, at a naval training base. It was a cold and rainy day. Before long, O'Kane and the *Tang*'s other surviving officers were reunited with the enlisted men and marched past fanatical-looking Japanese trainees who were practicing with bayonets, lunging back and forth. The Americans were made to sit alongside a wall near a building. Suddenly, they spotted a group of Japanese officers walking toward them.

A tall rear admiral began to inspect the row of miserable survivors, stopping in front of Bill Leibold, who was sitting next to Dick O'Kane.

The rear admiral looked down at Leibold.

"Are you frightened?" he asked in excellent English.

Leibold was shivering badly from the cold.

"No, I'm cold."

The rear admiral looked at him contemptuously.

"Of course you're cold, stupid! You've got no shoes!"

Leibold tried to ask for some dry clothes.

The rear admiral ignored the request and then asked Leibold how old he was.

"Twenty-one."

The rear admiral looked skeptical.

"You're not a day under thirty-five."

The rear admiral then turned to O'Kane and asked his age.

O'Kane replied that he was in fact thirty-three.

"No, you're not," said the rear admiral, seeming to take delight in pointing out how quickly the *Tang*'s survivors were aging under such extreme duress.

"You're at least fifty."[27]

That concluded the inspection. The rear admiral and his party walked away. "We had no clothing to speak of," recalled Leibold. "It was a miserable time. I figured they were going to give us shoes and clothes, but they didn't give us anything."[28]

The *Tang* survivors were then loaded onto a small boat and taken across a bay to a train station. O'Kane vividly remembered the ensuing journey northward to Yokohama, a major industrial center: "The countryside may have been beautiful, but the fast, loaded trains, the hydro-electric lines coming down out of the mountains, and the buzzing industry were depressing to us."

O'Kane realized how formidable an enemy Japan really was. "It was dark, but the factories were booming like Kaiser's shipyards, with the bluish light of arc-welding spread out through the city. And here I knew that Japan, with her routes to China quite defensible, could be defeated only by invasion."[29]

The journey seemed to last a long time. Finally, the train came to a standstill. It was late at night. They were herded onto a bus, which wound up into hills, and then marched along a muddy road for several miles. Their muscles ached. A steady rain soaked them to the bone. They had been given no coats. Jesse DaSilva had no shoes or shirt. He was especially cold and his feet were sore and numb.

Finally, the *Tang*'s nine survivors reached a set of gates and were lined up in front of them. They had arrived at perhaps the most brutal of all POW camps on mainland Japan. The camp had earned its nickname: "Torture Farm."[30]

11

Torture Farm

THE *Tang* survivors had reached the gates of a secret naval intelligence interrogation center known as Ofuna, situated on the southern outskirts of Yokohama. For a while, they stood and shivered in the cold. "The only thing I had on was a pair of dungarees," recalled Jesse DaSilva. "I had lost one of my sandals after we were torpedoed and I kicked the other one off before I escaped [from the *Tang*], so my feet were very sore and numb from the cold." Pete Narowanski was still wearing his swimming trunks and Hawaiian shirt.[1]

Ofuna was built in a U-shape with the Japanese guards' quarters in the middle and prisoners' barracks on each side of a fence. The most recent arrivals were kept on one side of the fence until they had been interrogated. As soon as they arrived, guards made it clear that the *Tang* survivors were not to speak with each other, and especially not with the prisoners on the other side of the fence.[2] If they did so, they would be beaten and made to sit in the infamous "Ofuna crouch," which meant "standing on the ball of your foot, knees half bent and arms extended over the head."[3]

Japanese guards took the *Tang* survivors into a holding room where they were each given a dry shirt and pants. "They [also handed out] a pair of tennis shoes that were three sizes too small," recalled DaSilva. "This was all the clothing I ever received the whole time I was a POW. They also gave us blankets."[4]

Then Caverly and Leibold were singled out and told by a guard to follow him to a galley. There, a U.S. Marine pilot handed them a bucket full of warm, lumpy rice and bowls.

The pilot was none other than Major Gregory "Pappy" Boying-ton—a future Medal of Honor recipient. Leibold recognized the hard-living, thirty-four-year-old Boyington immediately, having recently read an article about him in a magazine that included a full-page picture of the soon-to-be legendary ace, credited with twenty-two kills. Boyington's famous escapades and derring-do would later inspire the hugely popular 1970s television series *Baa Baa Black Sheep*.

Unknown to Leibold, Boyington was recovering from losing eighty pounds since being shot down on January 3, 1944, and then being fished out of the water by the crew of a Japanese subma-rine. He had befriended a Japanese grandmother, who worked in the camp's kitchen and helped him pilfer food.[5]

Leibold and Caverly took the food back and placed bowls of rice and tea in front of their fellow survivors' cells in a section of the camp called Ekku. Each man had been given his own cell, six feet long by ten feet wide, with a barred window at one end and a raised floor with a three-by-six-foot mat at the other.

The next morning, the men learned that they would not be afforded any of the rights of other POWs.[6] "They told us they were classifying us as special prisoners of Japan," recalled Clay Decker. "They contended that ninety percent of the crews of merchant ships were civilians so we were waging war against their civilian population. We were not entitled to be POWs. We [would] only get half the food rations. They [had not] notified the Red Cross that we were captured."[7]

Because they were submariners, the *Tang* survivors were particularly at risk. As one of the camp's interrogators had already explained to another submariner in the camp: "You have survived the sinking of a submarine. No one survives the sinking of a submarine. No one knows you're alive. We are going to ask you questions. This man and this man are going to shoot you if you don't answer the questions, and no one will ever know you were alive."[8]

There was at least some pleasant news. "On the nicer side was word that we would start learning Japanese on the following day," recalled O'Kane. "Discounting the threats, the opportunity to learn a foreign language seemed a fair exchange. . . . We at least had a chance to live."[9]

The *Tang* survivors would always remember the Japanese lesson they received the following day. The Japanese had decided to make an example of some of the older prisoners. They were going to show the new arrivals what would happen if they didn't cooperate during interrogation. "We were not there very long when they opened the gates between the two compounds and had the older prisoners lined up facing the guards," recalled Jesse DaSilva.[10]

The survivors watched as Lieutenant Commander J. A. Fitzgerald, captain of the *Grenadier,* and two other emaciated men were then selected for punishment.[11]

Fitzgerald had been forced to scuttle his boat after it had been bombed on April 23, 1943, some eighteen months before the *Tang* survivors had been picked up.[12] Of the submarine officers in Ofuna, who numbered perhaps a couple of dozen, Fitzgerald had been treated the worst, enduring excruciating torture on an almost daily basis. According to Vice Admiral Lockwood, this had included "beatings, water cures, and standing at attention or in strained positions—hands over heads with knees bent—for hours on end . . . clubs, pencils between the fingers, the blade of a penknife shoved underneath the fingernails. . . . The water cure given to Fitzgerald consisted of tying him face up on a bench with his head hanging over the end. Then his feet were elevated and water poured from a teakettle into his nostrils. A hand over his mouth forced him to swallow the water, and when he was judged to be sufficiently full of water, a club beating would be administered. Usually he became unconscious during this last torture, whereupon they would revive him and try questioning again. When this was unsuccessful, another clubbing followed. The miracle is that he survived and kept his reason."[13]

Now Fitzgerald and others were to be beaten to within a breath of life. Three of the biggest guards stepped forward. One grabbed a club and went to work, beating Fitzgerald and the others across the buttocks. The bat swung through the air until the men could take the beating no more and collapsed. Caverly was so disgusted that he vomited. "It made me sick when they beat Fitzgerald and those guys," he remembered.[14]

"After watching this I knew what could be expected if we didn't do what we were told," recalled Jesse DaSilva.[15]

Fitzgerald was knocked into unconsciousness. Other guards were not satisfied, however, and grabbed the men who had collapsed and held them up so they could be beaten some more. The stunned *Tang* survivors were then marched back to their cells while the head guard proceeded to kick the three men, even though they were out cold.

O'Kane and his men believed, incorrectly as it turned out, that the men had been beaten to death.[16] It was a terrifying introduction to Ofuna, where the most primitive methods were used to extract information from men whom the Japanese considered to be war criminals.

THEN IT BEGAN. On their third day in Ofuna, the *Tang* survivors were summoned one by one for interrogation. O'Kane had advised them to cooperate with the Japanese: "Anything the Japs ask you, answer them. Don't tell them a lie. Don't let them catch you in a lie. Anything that you know, you can rest assured they already know. I'm the guy they're after."[17]

Jesse DaSilva may have been the first to be questioned. He was taken to a small room with a table and two chairs. A Japanese officer sat opposite DaSilva. "He was very polite and could speak very good English," recalled DaSilva. "He would offer me a cigarette and ask me how everything was. He told me he had been educated in the U.S. He would ask me the same questions over and over as I would give him the same answers [that] he would not accept. Then he let me leave. This only happened a few times. I guess he figured I didn't know anything."[18]

The interrogators were young and spoke English; some had been students in America. One said he had been to the University of Arkansas. Known as the "quiz kids" by the American prisoners, they were skilled interrogators, trained by the Imperial Japanese Navy's general staff, and they came out to Ofuna on a daily basis from their headquarters at the Yokosuka naval base. The youngest of the three, known to some of the prisoners as "Handsome Harry" because of his clean-cut looks, smart suit, and polished shoes, had worked from 1934 to 1941 in the office of the Japanese naval attaché in Washington.

Floyd Caverly tried to convince his interrogators that he knew very little about the technical aspects of the *Tang*'s operations—that he was in fact a "dumb-head."[19] Of course, his knowledge of the latest techniques in sonar and radar made him, after O'Kane, the most important source of potentially crucial information. So when he was asked about his role on the *Tang*, Caverly said that his main responsibility was to replace broken lightbulbs and fuses after a depth-charging.

What was Caverly's rating?

Caverly explained that he was a *Dinkyshuzinski*—a light-bulb repairman.

Caverly was shown an instruction book for the *Tang*'s radar.

"I don't understand those books too well," replied Caverly. "I don't read too well."

And so it went on until finally the interrogator looked at the guards in the room in frustration.

"Get him the hell out of here."[20]

All the *Tang* survivors said that depth-charging had been the cause of the *Tang*'s loss. They also let the Japanese believe that they were part of a wolf pack. This was crucial. Indeed, if the Japanese knew that the *Tang* alone had sunk so many ships on the night of October 24–25, they might have quickly paid with their lives or, at the very least, been beaten like Fitzgerald.

When Larry Savadkin's turn came, he tried to confuse his interrogators with false information: "I just kept telling the interrogators I was a 'prospective' engineering officer. I really didn't know much about the submarine. It didn't seem to matter what you told the questioner, just so they could keep filling out papers to send back to Tokyo. I made the wildest statements about [the] speed and power of our ship. My machinist made wild statements in the other direction."[21]

When Clay Decker and Jesse DaSilva were then asked about Savadkin's statements, one of them replied: "Well, you know, Mr. Savadkin—just a greenhorn, doesn't know a thing."[22]

AS WITH CAPTAIN FITZGERALD of the *Grenadier*, special treatment was reserved for the *Tang*'s Dick O'Kane. When asked how many ships he had sunk, O'Kane said five from five patrols. His interrogators at first appeared to be satisfied by this answer. But then they found a newspaper report on the *Tang*. O'Kane was brought back for further questioning. A sergeant was soon standing before O'Kane, wielding a club the size of a baseball bat.

"We have some good news for you," said an interrogating officer. "The army football team beat the navy today. . . . And we have some other news . . . about the USS *Tang*."

"Oh, is that right?" replied O'Kane.

"Yes, it just got awarded the presidential unit citation for sinking 110,000 tons."

It was obvious—the *Tang* had sunk far more than five Japanese ships. And now the Japanese knew it. The sergeant lashed out and O'Kane was quickly clubbed unconscious.

At some point, O'Kane regained his senses.

Floyd Caverly was huddling up for warmth when he heard O'Kane talking to a guard as he was brought back to his cell. O'Kane knew the guard could not understand what he was saying, but he wanted his men to overhear him.

"Hey, we were awarded the unit citation."

Caverly heard, as did the others. For a while at least, the news managed to lift their spirits.[23]

THE BITE OF WINTER was in the air. It was mid-November and the *Tang* survivors felt the cold all the more because of their inadequate clothing.[24]

The highlight of their first weeks in captivity was a hot bath, by now the only thing that managed to get any feeling back in Jesse Da Silva's frostbitten feet.[25] But bath time was not so pleasant for some men who were singled out for humiliation. Bill Leibold would vividly recall Hayes Trukke being picked on: "The Japanese had placed curtains over the showers but they pulled them aside. We were naked. Trukke had a large penis, and they all pointed to it."[26] Floyd Caverly also remembered the incident: "He was pretty well-hung for a little guy. They'd point at him and then they'd point at me and say, 'Look at that little bastard.'"[27]

But it was at night, when drunken guards would roam Ofuna's corridors looking for "sport," that the men were most abused.[28] "The guards would sneak in and whack you with a club when you were sound asleep," recalled Floyd Caverly. "They didn't give a damn where they hit you. Sometimes they'd even hit you in the back of the head and knock you cold. One night I was beaten. Two vertebrae got cracked."[29]

The guards' favorite weapon was a cherry club shaped like a baseball bat. After interrogation, if the *Tang* survivors had not been cooperative, recalled Bill Leibold, "a mark was made on your cell door. You could expect a 'visit' by one of two guards with [clubs] during the night. . . . Mistreatment was a daily affair."[30]

Those with the toughest backgrounds, such as Pete Narowanski, seemed to hold up fairly well. But no matter how resilient they were, the men knew they could last only so long. They could see it in one another's sallow, jaundiced features; in the bloated joints caused by beriberi; in the yellow, rotting teeth of friends who no longer smiled. They were slowly wasting away, losing strength and stamina ounce by ounce, as all men do who have been placed on a starvation diet.[31]

BACK IN AMERICA that November, the *Tang* survivors' families waited for news from their loved ones. They did not know yet that the *Tang* was reported missing.

Fellow U.S. submariners were, by contrast, already in mourning. "We of the submarine force grieved silently . . . at the news that *Tang* was no more," recalled Ned Beach, who would write several best-selling books about the Silent Service, including the classic *Run Silent, Run Deep*. "With submarines, this news is not the sudden receipt of specific information; it is the gradual realization that it is a day or two since a certain boat should have reported in from patrol."

The submarine force knew early on that the *Tang* had disappeared, but not what had happened to her and the crew. Rumors started to circulate. The *Tang* had attacked a large convoy in shallow water. The *Tang* had battled several destroyers escorting the convoy. She had sunk many ships but had been caught in the open in shallow water. She had attacked several boats in a harbor while on the surface at night and had been sunk by shore batteries.

Murray Frazee, who had been the *Tang*'s executive officer on her first four patrols, was working in Pearl Harbor that winter. Through various intelligence sources, he discovered that the *Tang* had been lost in enemy action. But he was also informed that codebreakers had learned that there had been survivors.[32] "I was told very confidentially by a senior officer," recalled Frazee, "who got the word from the intelligence staff . . . that the *Tang* had been sunk by her own torpedo, only nine of the eighty-seven-man crew survived, and that O'Kane was a prisoner of war."

Frazee longed to tell O'Kane's wife, Ernestine, but he decided not to. To prevent the Japanese from realizing that the Allies had broken their codes, Frazee could not say a word. It was an agonizing decision that would haunt him to the end of his life. "All I could do was bite my tongue," he recalled. "If the Japanese ever suspected that we were breaking their codes, they would have changed everything, and we would be back at square one. So Ernie O'Kane . . . had to suffer."[33]

Ernestine and her family, and the wives and families of eight other men, could not know that there was reason for hope. They could not know that they should wait until the end of the war, that there was at least a slim chance that their son or lover or father or husband was still alive and might one day turn up on their front porch.

The decision to remain silent must have been particularly difficult. As executive officer, Frazee had also been mail censor on the first four of the *Tang*'s patrols, and he knew of the men's families, about their children and their private lives. Perhaps to ease his anguish, Frazee would later send a letter describing the qualities of each man aboard to the families of the *Tang*'s crew. It was the least he could do.

THAT THANKSGIVING OF 1944, there seemed precious little to be grateful for. Indeed, it was a terribly sad time for the relatives and wives who finally learned that the *Tang* had gone missing.

In Los Angeles, Bill Leibold's family was traumatized by the news that he was presumed lost at sea. However, his young wife, Grace, and his father were steadfast in their belief that he was still alive.[34] Across town, Jesse DaSilva's relatives were not so convinced and decided to hold a memorial service for him at their Lutheran church.[35]

Over sixty years later, Jackie Narowanski, only four years old when news of the *Tang*'s fate arrived, would vividly recall being summoned into a front room by her grandmother, Anya, who also called for her eldest daughter, Sophie. When Sophie arrived, Anya handed her a Western Union telegram. She wanted Sophie to read it out to the family; she herself could not read.

Sophie read the telegram. Peter, Anya's favorite son, was missing in action. The family broke down. Then Anya calmed the room, insisting that everyone kneel at the window; they were to ask God to allow her son to make it home. Four year-old Jackie kneeled and prayed until she could pray no more and then fell asleep. The next thing she knew, her grandmother was soothing her and telling her everything would be all right.

"Your father is okay," she said. "He will come home. I can see him . . . he's alive . . . in the water."[36]

MOTHER OF TWO, Ernestine O'Kane received a Western Union telegram at her two-bedroom apartment in the Bay Area:

WASHINGTON D.C.

THE NAVY DEPARMENT DEEPLY REGRETS TO INFORM YOU THAT YOUR HUSBAND COMMANDER RICHARD HETHERINGTON O'KANE USN IS MISSING FOLLOWING ACTION WHILE IN THE

SERVICE OF HIS COUNTRY. THE DEPARTMENT APPRECIATES YOUR
GREAT ANXIETY BUT DETAILS NOT AVAILABLE NOW AND DELAY
IN RECEIPT THEREOF MUST NECESSARILY BE EXPECTED. TO
PREVENT POSSIBLE AID TO OUR ENEMIES AND TO SAFEGUARD
THE LIVES OF OTHER PERSONNEL PLEASE DO NOT DIVULGE THE
NAME OF HIS SHIP OR STATION OR DISCUSS PUBLICLY THE FACT
THAT HE IS MISSING.[37]

Ernestine was devastated, but she was also a woman of remarkable courage and faith. Immediately, she contacted other
Tang wives and tried to give them hope. There was a chance that
the men were still alive. They could be POWs. It was possible to
survive the sinking of a submarine. In the following months, she
kept in touch, sending out a newsletter and many more letters, all
of them intended to give comfort to the families of the men who
had not returned.

Not long after the official telegram announcing that her husband was missing, Ernestine received a letter from Vice Admiral
Lockwood. O'Kane, wrote Lockwood, had been "the heart and
soul of the ship. His leadership, his coolness under counter-
attack, his daring, his determination to destroy any and all enemy
ships encountered, all combined to make him the idol of his fellow skippers and of his seniors."[38]

Lockwood gave no indication that O'Kane was still alive. Yet he
had already learned from intelligence sources that this was the
case.[39] To protect the secret of Ultra, he, too, had to remain silent.

IT WAS ALREADY TWO FEET DEEP, and the snow kept falling.
They could see it piling up as they peered through the cracks in

their cell walls, as they huddled under their thin blankets, their stomachs cramping from hunger, their fingers and toes numb from the drafts that blasted them whenever the wind blew.

Winter had arrived in Japan. Because there was no other means of keeping the inmates warm, the guards decided to let the prisoners into the Ofuna compound for an hour each day so they could at least exercise to stay warm. "The only clothing we had was what we had on our backs," recalled DaSilva, "so we would march around with blankets over our heads and stamp our feet to get the circulation going. There we were, all walking around in a circle with blankets over our heads looking like a bunch of old Mother Hubbards."[40]

Enlisted man Floyd Caverly often walked in circles with his captain, Dick O'Kane.[41] Rank had barely separated the men before and did not matter a jot now. "O'Kane would tell me about little Marsha, his daughter, and his family," recalled Caverly. "I would listen to him and sympathize. He also talked about Jim, his son."

Floyd Caverly also often walked around the exercise yard with the tough, bony-faced Irishman, Hank Flanagan, whose lean features were increasingly cadaverous.

"You know, if we do live through this," Flanagan told Caverly, "and I get back to the States, I'm not taking any shit off anybody. I don't care if it's my old lady or relatives or friends or whoever."

He would be true to his word.[42]

AS THE WEEKS PASSED, the *Tang* survivors became increasingly concerned about their families. Had they been told of their fate? Those with young wives worried that they might be seeing new men. It was likely that some had given up hope and begun to get on with their lives. After all, no one had so far returned to the States after their submarine had been reported missing. Only in Ofuna had the *Tang* veterans discovered that a few other very fortunate men, such as Lieutenant Commander Fitzgerald's crew from the *Grenadier,* had survived the loss of their submarines.[43]

During their months at sea, the *Tang* survivors had listened to Japanese propaganda, in particular Tokyo Rose's broadcasts, and often laughed. "We had heard her on the radio," recalled Floyd Caverly. "She had said things like: 'You knuckleheads, why don't you give up this damned war and go home . . . who do you suppose is dancing with your wife at night? Are you going to have a girlfriend when you get home? I don't think so.'"[44]

Now Tokyo Rose's warnings returned to haunt the *Tang* survivors. Seven of the nine were married. Their wives were for the most part in their early twenties. Would they remain faithful?

They were right to be worried. Sadly, only three of the *Tang*'s survivors would still be married by the end of 1945. Unknown to Larry Savadkin, his young wife, Sarah, was already sleeping with a new man in Rochester, New York; she would soon become pregnant with the man's child.[45] Clay Decker's wife, Lucille, the mother of his two-year-old son, Harry, had also given up hope of him returning. She too would soon fall in love with a new man.

12

The Coldest Winter

DECEMBER 1944 in Ofuna was a bleak month. The men were heartened briefly by the appearance of silver-winged B-29 planes over the camp, headed to bomb nearby cities, but there was precious little else to lift their spirits. Just before Christmas, they were joined by five of the crew of the British submarine H.M.S. *Strategem*. Several B-29 pilots also became prisoners. Then, at Christmas, the Red Cross delivered food parcels.[1] Finally, it seemed, there was reason to celebrate.

"Several guards came," recalled Bill Leibold, "opened our cell doors, and gave each of us a Red Cross food package." The packages contained the stuff of dreams: soap, cigarettes, gum, a chocolate bar, powdered milk, dried prunes or raisins, canned fish and meat, a small block of cheese, and a can opener.[2] "We were ordered not to open or use any of the contents as we were going outside to celebrate our Christmas with other prisoners. We were to leave the packages in our cells."

The *Tang* survivors were taken outside. A gate was opened and prisoners from the other parts of the camp were allowed into the compound where the *Tang* men were being held in solitary confinement. From the other men, the *Tang* survivors learned that the *Grenadier*'s captain, John Fitzgerald, had in fact survived the brutal beating the day after their arrival. Leibold also had a chance to chat with Major Pappy Boyington for the first time since the day he had served them rice.

After an hour, the survivors were returned to their cells. To their outrage they found that their Red Cross packages had been stolen or were emptied of valuable goods. The men were furious and began to protest loudly. "We all did a lot of shouting and beating on our cell doors," recalled Leibold. "The guard was concerned about the racket we were making and finally showed up with a basket of hot sweet potatoes. He gave two potatoes to us."

The men quickly devoured the potatoes. At least there had been something other than their pitiful ration of hard rice with which to celebrate Christmas.

THE YEAR 1944 finally drew to a close. It had been a triumphant twelve months for the submarine force operating in the Pacific. Lockwood's underwater raiders had sunk 548 vessels and the Japanese had lost so many fuel tankers that supplying their forces in Empire waters had become a desperate struggle. Thousands of Japanese soldiers and sailors had also been killed as American submarines had carried out unrestricted warfare with a vengeance.

Captains of O'Kane's ilk and caliber had struck at the heart of the Japanese military colossus and crippled it.[3]

In the first months of the new year, the rate of sinking would rapidly decrease—so few ships were left to sink. To all intents and purposes, the submarine war was drawing to a close. It had been a remarkably lethal and effective campaign.[4]

JANUARY 1945 SAW THE SKIES above Ofuna fill with more and more B-29s. But it also saw many men begin to die. O'Kane discovered that he was suffering from ulcers caused by scurvy. To his dismay, they would not heal.[5]

However, the new year also brought a long-awaited change to the survivors' routine. The men were transferred to the other side of the fence in Ofuna and they no longer had to suffer solitary confinement. They could now take care of each other and pool greater resources to help the weaker men.

A few weeks later, the harsh conditions finally took their toll— the first man to die was twenty-four-year-old Lieutenant Richard L. Hunt, on February 25, 1945. He had been brought into the camp on January 17, bandaged from head to foot, suffering from terrible burns caused when the B-29 he was in crashed.[6] Unable to use his hands to feed himself, he starved to death.

Dick O'Kane had protested to the Japanese, demanding that he and other *Tang* survivors be allowed to feed and care for Hunt.[7] By the time the Japanese agreed to O'Kane's request, Hunt was as good as dead. Nevertheless, the *Tang*'s survivors did what they could to help ease Hunt's pain. "I was given the impossible task of washing his bandages," recalled Bill Leibold. "He deteriorated to a point where the guards would not go into his cell due to the stench."

Not long after, Hunt died. Bill Leibold and others carried his remains to a small wooden building, which served as Ofuna's morgue. Late one night, Hunt was buried across a road from the camp in a makeshift graveyard.[8]

Jesse DaSilva had volunteered to join the burial party, knowing he would receive a boiled potato in return. They had to carry the corpse through deep snow to a hilly wooded area. They then dug a hole and buried the young flyer, about 180 yards north of Ofuna, in the rear of a nearby temple called Ryuhoji Temple.

It was later thought that Hunt was injected with poison by the camp doctor, perhaps to put him out of his misery given the absence of proper medicine and painkillers.[9]

MEANWHILE, BACK IN THE STATES, more families were receiving official confirmation that their loved ones from the *Tang* were missing. Floyd Caverly's wife, Leone, received a letter from the navy explaining that "The USS *Tang* was conducting an offensive war patrol against the enemy in the Empire waters. In that she did not return as scheduled, and no word has been heard from her, nor any information concerning the possibility of her survivors, it is regrettable that all officers and men are considered missing."[10]

The letter included a list with each man's next of kin. Twenty-four of the men were married. Twenty-three other women were now also concluding that their husbands had in all likelihood been lost.

All over America, such telegrams were arriving in unprecedented numbers. The war was bloodier, more costly than ever, and Americans were beginning to tire of the slaughter. In January, over twenty thousand Americans had been killed in the European Theater alone. To defeat Japan, hundreds of thousands more were expected to become casualties.

IN OFUNA, LATE IN FEBRUARY, the *Tang's* survivors got their first real jolt of hope that the war might end before they had wasted away. They saw Avenger bombers from an aircraft carrier fly over and strike targets in Japan. "The [attack] signified to us that the Philippines were secure," recalled O'Kane, "for otherwise our carriers could not be this far north. As before, a glance to the skies meant a beating from the guards, but the sight of torpedo bombers just yards away was worth it."[11]

More and more bombers soon filled the skies, wreaking greater destruction. With the same escalating intensity, malnutrition took its toll on the inmates of Ofuna. Beriberi was rampant. According to O'Kane, four prisoners died of the disease in March alone, and many more, including Larry Savadkin, were soon barely able to walk. Men throughout Ofuna got weaker by the hour it seemed, having expended their last resources of fat and energy.

Every one of the survivors was now focused on just one objective: finding enough food to stay alive, no matter what form it came in, stolen or otherwise. Obtaining extra nutrition, any kind, was all that mattered. As they were learning, the alternative was death.

To compound the brutal psychological effects of slow starvation, some of the Japanese guards would flaunt choice items from the Red Cross packages they had raided. It made the prisoners' blood boil, sending some close to the edge of insanity as they lay awake at night, their stomachs cramping, shivering even as the nights got warmer because most had no body fat left to act as insulation. Once proud physiques were now reduced to skin and bone and their muscles atrophied to the point of immobility.

Bill Leibold and Floyd Caverly, having kept each other alive in the water when the *Tang* went down, now conspired to keep each other from dying of starvation. One day, the pair was cleaning a passageway when they came across what appeared to be a locked storeroom. There was no guard in sight, so they forced a sliding door off its track. Inside were stacks of Red Cross packages, boxes that had been withheld from the men in the camp. It was an infuriating discovery. Had the men been given the parcels, they would have been in far better shape.

Suddenly, a guard appeared at the end of the passageway. Leibold and Caverly staged a fight, Leibold punching Caverly. Caverly fell against the door. The guard broke up the fight and railed at them for knocking the door open.

A few nights later, Caverly and Leibold snuck out of their cells, lifting planks in the floor, and returned to the stash of Red Cross boxes. Using stolen side cutters, they opened a large box bound with wire. "We took two small boxes and switched the large box to the bottom of the stack with unopened boxes on top."[12] The other inmates were soon doing likewise.

Eventually, the camp authorities discovered that the confiscated boxes had been raided. Punishment was sure to come. On April 5, after breakfast, the *Tang* survivors and others were lined up in front of their barracks and accused of stealing the boxes. Leibold, Caverly, and others responsible did not confess.

The Japanese made the men stand at attention. "We stayed this way all day without lunch," recalled Jesse DaSilva. "Come dinner time, they made us get into a pushup position and if anyone moved, a guard would hit them with a club across the buttocks.

This didn't seem to work so they took us back inside the barracks and lined us up in the center and asked again who was responsible. Still no answer. Then the guards took turns and whacked us across the buttocks with a large club several times each. Still no answer."[13]

Not one of the men cracked under the strain. Finally, their silence and their solidarity forced their tormentors to relent.

A FEW DAYS LATER, the *Tang* survivors learned to their enormous relief that they were going to be sent to a regular POW camp. Nearly five months of hell in the "Torture Farm" were over. Because of the influx of downed B-29 pilots and other new POWs who needed to be interrogated, the camp administration had decided to transfer them to another camp in the Tokyo area.

Major Boyington was selected as the leader of a group of transferees that included all of the *Tang*'s enlisted men.[14] On April 6, Boyington led these men out of Ofuna, under armed guard, toward a train.[15] As he left the "Torture Farm," Boyington looked back one last time at the squalid camp. At last, he could turn his back on a place that he would always remember as being full of pain—and ugly. "I wasn't conscious of the [surrounding] quiet wooded scenery," he recalled. "I saw no beauty [there]."[16]

Some of the men in Boyington's charge were dressed in rags. Others could barely walk. But they all summoned the necessary energy to march away from Ofuna. At the nearby railway station, they took a tram to Yokohama. They then walked through the ruined city to an area known as Omori on the western shore of Tokyo Bay. When they crossed a long wooden causeway that led to a small man-made island, they entered another, larger POW camp.

Omori means "great forest" in Japanese, but precious few trees were on the island when the Americans arrived. "It was mostly sand," recalled one of the prisoners. "The camp, surrounded by a six-foot fence, took up most of the island. On the other side of the fence [there were] big holes in the 'beach,' where the prisoners charged with cleaning the latrines dumped the human excrement. Thousands of flies hovered over this sickening, open sewer."[17]

Until the war was over—or until they died—the stench of feces would engulf them. For the lucky POWs who would survive, the smell would never leave them, seeping into their very consciousness it seemed, a constant reminder of how worthless they were in the eyes of the Japanese.

13

The Last Stretch

O MORI'S COMMANDANT walked into the open ground at the center of the camp and addressed the new arrivals. They were war criminals, he explained, so they were going to be kept separate from the other prisoners in the camp. If the Japanese lost the war, they would be executed. With that, guards marched the new inmates to their new home.[1]

Many of the men were relieved to find out that they would not return to solitary confinement, even in this new camp. Solitary confinement was a punishment, as they had learned, harsher even than random beatings or slow starvation.

The men were in a pitiful condition as they settled into their new "home," a flimsy, cramped barracks with a dirt floor and wooden platforms for sleeping. Jesse DaSilva remembered that all of the *Tang* survivors now suffered from diarrhea. Several had beriberi, caused by lack of B vitamins; the most painful symptoms were cramping of the thighs, extreme soreness in the leg muscles, and a burning sensation in the feet. Their daily sustenance was half a cup of low-grade rice and a small bowl of watery soup, served at breakfast, lunch, and supper. There was no meat, no source of life-saving protein or essential vitamins to prevent diseases such as beriberi and scurvy.[2]

Dick O'Kane was in the worst shape. And his men were increasingly concerned. Wracked by pain in his feet from beriberi, suffering from jaundice and painfully thin, he was so exhausted by the daily battle to survive that he even let his stubble grow. On the *Tang*, he had railed against facial hair of any kind, but now that priorities had changed, foraging for food seemed more important than whiskers. "He grew the prettiest red beard you ever saw," recalled Floyd Caverly.[3]

O'Kane was at least grateful to be out of Ofuna. He was no longer being beaten, tortured, and questioned endlessly about the *Tang*. He later explained that the change to Omori was "like surfacing after an all-day dive." But the fact remained that he and the other *Tang* survivors were still extraordinarily vulnerable. The men were still "special prisoners" and not registered as POWs with the Red Cross. No one would be the wiser if, on some dark night, they were taken out into the ruins of Yokohama and shot, their bodies disappearing into a vast, rubble-strewn graveyard. And if they were not killed in a fit of vengeance by their guards, they would surely not escape the fate of so many Japanese civilians, being bombed night after night.

A week after the men arrived in Omori, there was a huge raid on Tokyo that lit up the entire bay and night sky. The firestorm could be seen by the prisoners. The following night, other cities were targeted—Yokohama, Omori, and Kawasaki. Shrapnel pinged off barrack roofs. Flimsy wooden homes nearby were raised in seconds. "When the fireworks started, the Japanese boarded up all the windows in the barracks, then they went to the air raid shelters," recalled Clay Decker. "We were left exposed. . . . It was frightening as bombs were dropping all around. Some fragments ended up in camp."[4]

The ground shook. Some of the prisoners could feel the heat from the massive fires caused by the raids. One saw a wall of fire, three hundred feet high, spreading for miles. Every factory in the area appeared to have been hit. "They bombed the hell out of the place," recalled Floyd Caverly. "We saw flames and then the smoke came. We damn near choked to death from the smoke."[5]

Pete Narowanski and a fellow prisoner managed to find an empty shelter. To their delight, they discovered some abandoned packages of noodles in there.[6] The bombing was good for one thing at least—it had bought Narowanski and his buddy a few more days of life.

When they woke the next morning, the prisoners saw that the nearby city of Omori lay in ruins. Even though the Omori camp was just eight hundred feet from the mainland, no bombs had fallen on the prison grounds.

THE SPECIAL PRISONERS, which included the *Tang* survivors, were kept inside Omori throughout April, while other prisoners left on daily work details. Major Boyington tried to persuade camp officials to allow the special prisoners to join the work gangs so they could, at least, "get out in the sunshine and get some exercise."⁷ The Japanese finally relented. And so, at the start of May 1945, the *Tang*'s crew crossed the causeway leading to the mainland and were put to work clearing bomb wreckage.⁸

They had a seemingly endless job ahead of them. By now, most of industrial Japan lay in smoldering ruins. And there was no sign of an end to the bombing. In just over a month, every major industrial city in Japan would be destroyed. Almost thirteen million Japanese would be homeless. Around two hundred Allied POWs would be killed in the raids.⁹ Perhaps a hundred B-29 pilots would be shot down and then brutally killed, often beheaded after extreme torture. The vast majority of victims, however, were the hundreds of thousands of civilians, most of them burned to death, often to cinders, in the most lethal bombing raids in history.

One morning, Clay Decker tagged along with Pappy Boyington on a work detail into a nearby area to clean up after the silver B-29s had dropped their loads. "Our boys would drop one incendiary bomb and it would knock seven blocks out, just like that," he recalled. "We loaded dead bodies on flatbed trucks, and then we'd clean up the areas. It gave us something to do. We were glad to do it."¹⁰

Pappy Boyington also persuaded the guards to let the men plant a vegetable garden in a bombed out area of nearby Yokohama. Since Jesse DaSilva was now too weak to perform hard labor, he volunteered to carry drinking water to the garden each day and distribute it to the men when they needed it.

"I remember once when one of the guys slipped off to the nearby fish market," he recalled. "I don't know where he got the money, but he bought some fish and I boiled them in the can of water. We tried to sneak them back into camp for our evening meal, but the smell of the cooked fish alerted the guards. They took the fish away and our group leaders were punished."¹¹

DaSilva also scoured ruins for "choice items" of discarded food like fish heads. "When you're starving, anything tastes good," he recalled. "One time we were all sitting around on our tea break when an old dog strayed by and we sat around discussing the possibility of eating it. But none of us had the heart to kill it."[12]

DaSilva couldn't stop thinking about the three apple pies in the *Tang*'s galley that he'd noticed as he rushed to the forward torpedo room. Pete Narowanski remembered the turkeys that were thawing for the Thanksgiving dinner that was to be held on their journey home. "I knew if I ever got back home, I'd never starve again," vowed DaSilva.[13]

BACK IN AMERICA, for at least one of the survivor's wives, there was suddenly reason for hope. An officer named Dusty Dornin, one of O'Kane's friends working in naval intelligence, decided to ease Ernestine O'Kane's misery. "He wrote that a garbled message had been received via radio listing some men as present in a prison camp in Japan," she recalled. "Among the names was a Jed O'King and the only person the U.S. files could come up with was . . . my husband."[14]

There was no doubt in Ernestine's mind. Her husband was alive.

14

Liberation

THE WAR WAS NEARING A CLIMAX. The Japanese appeared to have only two choices—surrender or die. At stake was unfathomable national pride: Never in its history had Japan been occupied by foreigners.

The nature of the men's work changed as it became clear that the Japanese were going to bunker down and resist until the last man, woman, and child. "About a month before the end of the war," recalled Pappy Boyington, "we were taken off our garden work and the clearing of debris and were set to digging huge tunnels in the hillsides on the outskirts of Yokohama. We worked at this twelve hours a day, just like [miners]. These tunnels were two hundred feet under the surface of the earth. One of the guards told me this was to be an air-raid shelter, but I couldn't imagine what kinds of bombs were going to be dropped to necessitate a tunnel two hundred feet underground."[1]

The inhabitants of Nagasaki and Hiroshima, two cities that had not yet been burned to cinders, were about to find out.

Unknown to the men in Omori, the Allies had decided at a conference code-named Terminal to try to force a quick end to the war. On July 26, the Japanese were ordered to surrender unconditionally or, they were warned, suffer "prompt and utter destruction."

The Japanese did not respond fast enough. On August 1, the utter destruction began: 836 B-29s—the largest number ever gathered in the air at one time—dropped more bombs on the cities of Honshu and Kyushu in one day than had ever been dropped in a twenty-four-hour period in history. Five days later, on August 6th, a B-29 bomber, named *Enola Gay*, dropped a single bomb called "Little Boy" on Hiroshima. More than a hundred thousand Japanese were killed, most horribly burned to death, others literally atomized.

The giant mushroom cloud had barely settled when President Harry Truman once more demanded surrender. Otherwise the Japanese would "face a rain of ruin from the air, the likes of which has never been seen on this earth." But still the Japanese fought on. Three days later, on August 9, another atomic bomb, "Fat Man," exploded over Nagasaki, killing about forty thousand civilians instantly, as well as over one hundred American POWs located in camps in and around the city.

Out of the ruins of Japan's incinerated cities now poured hundreds of thousands of refugees, looking for somewhere to hide from America's "rain of ruin," places like the mines where O'Kane and the *Tang* survivors were working—the last shelters for the seemingly condemned populace.

ALL THAT MORNING, radio broadcasts instructed the Japanese people to gather and listen to a speech from their emperor at noon. It would be the first time they would hear his voice. Listeners were instructed to stand during the broadcast.

At noon on August 15, most of Japan gathered around radio sets. They heard the national anthem, then a strange voice spoke in an old-fashioned language that many ordinary Japanese found hard to understand.

In the caves being dug on the mainland, across the causeway from Omori, Dick O'Kane and other survivors also listened as Emperor Hirohito's voice was broadcast over a public address system.

Hirohito began by stating that the terms offered by the Allies for surrender had been accepted and then gave several reasons why this had been done. "The enemy," he added, "had begun to employ a new and most cruel bomb, the power of which to do damage is indeed incalculable, taking the toll of many innocent lives. Should we continue to fight it would not only result in the ultimate collapse and obliteration of the Japanese nation, but also it would lead to the total extinction of human civilization. . . . We have resolved to pave the way for a grand peace for all the generations to come by enduring the unendurable and suffering the insufferable."[2]

Dick O'Kane and the *Tang* survivors understood one thing. The war was over.[3] They could tell by the expressions of the Japanese gathered around the public address system. It was clear from the looks of defeat on their faces and their hunched shoulders that Japan had surrendered.

Anxious moments followed. Would the guards take out their defeat on the prisoners? Thankfully, they were too stunned to react violently. The *Tang*'s survivors laid down their tools and returned to the Omori camp.

Senso ōwari.

The war is over.

That night, according to O'Kane, "The Japanese slaughtered an old horse at Omori and carted it with them as they went over the hill. But our resourceful cooks scrubbed out the intestines, [and] chopped them up."[4] Celebrating that night, the survivors feasted on corn and horse-gut stew. Victory tasted sweet.

The celebration did not last long. Later that night, some drunken guards, plastered on sake, threatened to kill all of the special prisoners, including the *Tang* crew. They yelled abuse and waved swords about. The seventeen special prisoners feared they would be beheaded in some ghastly orgy of killing meant to avenge Japan's defeat.

A sympathetic guard—one of the few who remained sober—tried to reassure the prisoners.

"The guards are getting very drunk," he said. "Some are threatening to kill all the American prisoners. Here's a hammer and some nails for you to nail your door closed. And don't worry because I'll protect you with my life—because that is my duty."

The doors were nailed shut. It wasn't long before the survivors recognized the drunken voice of a Japanese guard.

"Let me at the captives," said the drunken guard. "I'm going to kill all of them. I'll prove to them that Japan is greater than the United States. Let me at them."

The survivors looked through the cracks in their cell walls. They could see the Japanese guard staggering around outside. The friendly guard tried to restrain him but he broke away from his grip and slashed the air with a double-handled samurai sword. He then began to beat on the survivors' cell door, trying to smash it open. Pappy Boyington stood, holding the hammer, ready to strike.[5] Finally, after some terrifying moments, the guard gave up and collapsed somewhere, dead drunk.

AMONG THE FREED ALLIED PRISONERS who had been so ritually abused, surprisingly little retribution was taken against their captors. Men who had fantasized for months about getting back at their Japanese tormentors were mostly too exhausted to summon the energy needed to inflict revenge. One of the senior Japanese officers at Omori complained that one of the prisoners had defecated in one of his boots and urinated in the other.[6] But this appeared to be the extent of any reprisals.

A different kind of bombing now began. American B-29s arrived to save the POWs from starvation, dropping fifty-five-gallon drums of food and supplies from just a few hundred feet. They dropped so many vegetables, recalled O'Kane, that the camp soon looked like a "giant salad."[7]

The friendly bombing was so intense at one point that POWs had to place a sign in the compound telling the pilots to drop the supplies outside the camp.[8] But still they dumped their loads in the Omori compound, forcing Boyington and some of the *Tang* survivors to take to an air-raid shelter one day.

"Why don't you stay out here and get some of this stuff?" a prisoner asked Boyington. "You can watch these things come down and they won't hit you."

"Nuts to that," replied Boyington. "After living through all I have, I'm damned if I'm going to be killed by being hit on the head by a crate of peaches."⁹

THEY WERE AMERICAN SHIPS. They were flying the Stars and Stripes. There was no mistaking them, even in the far distance, across Tokyo Bay. It was August 28 when the men in Omori saw salvation arrive in the form of a destroyer task group, led by Commander Harold Stassen. As the ships came closer and finally anchored off Omori at dusk, they knew, finally, that rescue was at hand.

Higgins boats soon approached the Omori camp. Pete Narowanski was standing on a pier wearing nothing but a loincloth as they neared the beach. When he smiled, his fellow survivors could see that several of his teeth caps had been knocked out under torture.

One man in the jubilant throng could not wait a moment longer. He dived into the sea and began to swim toward his liberators. But fifty yards from the shore his atrophied muscles gave out and he needed to be saved. His head had been shaved, so Stassen's men grabbed him by the ears to yank him out of the water.¹⁰

The Higgins boats pulled up onto the beach. Men disembarked and some of them planted flags into the sand. Three flags unfurled slowly—the Dutch, British, and American. Boyington and many others saluted their respective national flags.

Navy photographers recorded other moving scenes. POWs waved homemade flags and cheered. Hundreds of men, including Jesse DaSilva and Clay Decker, climbed up on the pilings of the wharf and began to shout and cheer. Others were soon swarming

around Stassen, the former governor of Minnesota, who had resigned his office in 1943 to serve in the navy.

"God sakes, we didn't know you were alive," said Stassen.[11]

An officer on Stassen's staff walked over toward Pete
Narowanksi and others.

"Alright boys, get ready– we're going home!" shouted the
young officer.

The Omori camp's most senior officer, a six-foot-four-inch
colonel, ran down to the beach, and over to Stassen.

"You can't do it," said the Japanese colonel. "I have no authority from Tokyo to let any of these people go."

Stassen grabbed the hulking Japanese by the front of his tunic
and lifted him off the ground.

"I have no need for orders from Tokyo to do what I want with
these American prisoners."[12]

In case Stassen hadn't settled the issue, one of his officers then
stuck his revolver in the colonel's face.

"This is your Tokyo!"[13]

NOT FAR AWAY, Clay Decker stood beside Floyd Caverly and Bill
Leibold, watching as more of Stassen's rescue force arrived on the
beach. "It was a great sight. It was a powerful moment," recalled
Caverly. "We had been looking forward to it for some time. We saw
our flag—which had been forbidden."

Decker turned to Caverly.

"Come on, the Higgins boats are here," said Decker. "We've got
to get down there. They're filming the liberation for newsreels."

Decker rushed off and was soon being filmed and photo-
graphed. Caverly did not follow him down to the boats at first. He

and some others had been taking care of a young POW who was lying on the ground nearby, close to death. Caverly wanted to make sure the man got some medical treatment.

"Let's move him out," said Leibold.

Caverly turned to the man. "The U.S. Navy is here," he told him. "They are rescuing us. We're going to get a stretcher for you."

The man appeared to understand.

Caverly and Leibold went down to the beach to find a stretcher. When they returned with stretcher in hand, it was too late—the other men had left the young POW unattended because they were so excited.[14] He had died.

"Let's get the hell out of here," said Leibold.

STASSEN WAS PLANNING to start evacuation the following day but the conditions in Omori were so deplorable that he began to move men off the island immediately, despite the fading light.

Dick O'Kane was so weak he could not walk without being helped. Someone found a litter for him and he was placed with other severe cases of malnutrition on a section of the beach.

A doctor and medics from Stassen's force began to examine the sickest men. The doctor had to determine who should be evacuated first. When he checked on O'Kane, he turned to some litter-bearers.

"We'll leave this one," said the doctor. "He's not going to make it."

Dick O'Kane had barely enough strength to speak.

"There's no way I'm staying here," he protested. "I've come this far . . . I'm going to make it the rest of the way."[15]

The doctor relented and O'Kane was among the first to be taken off the beach.

Throughout the night and into the next day, men were evacuated to the ships of the Third Fleet now gathering in Tokyo Bay for the formal surrender, which was to take place on September 2, 1945. So began an intoxicating transition, from hell to heaven for many men: "Coffee and doughnuts and ice cream and Coke from Red Cross girls . . . white hospital ships, shining bright, with wonderful names, *Samaritan, Hope, Benevolence* . . . filthy prison camp clothes stripped off for burning . . . stinking bodies into the hot shower . . . the clean sweet scent of American soap, a delousing with DDT, penicillin for whatever might ail them, fresh new clothes—white men again in a white world."[16]

Floyd Caverly and Bill Leibold were separated but were later reunited on the same hospital ship, the USS *Benevolence*, as were Clay Decker and Jesse DaSilva.[17] They were given quick medical examinations and then sent to a mess hall to eat. "We ate until we got sick," recalled Caverly, "and we heaved it up and turned right around and went back down to that crazy chow line again."[18]

Only one of the *Tang*'s survivors was in critical condition—their captain, Richard O'Kane. He was drifting in and out of consciousness in a stateroom on the USS *Benevolence*. The doctors gave him only a fifty-fifty chance of making it.

Bill Leibold first learned from a pharmacist's mate that O'Kane was on board.

"Where's he at?" asked Leibold.

The pharmacist's mate took Leibold to O'Kane's room, where he was being fed intravenously. There was an empty bunk in the room. Leibold decided to stay with O'Kane, using the spare bunk.

Leibold was not able to stay long with his captain. He was told by navy personnel that he was to be evacuated back to the States by air.

"What about the skipper here?" asked Leibold.

"We can't move him yet."

Leibold did not want to leave O'Kane on his own. But he also wanted to go home. He tried to talk to O'Kane but without success—the captain was too weak and too heavily sedated. Leibold was unable to say goodbye and left reluctantly, thinking he might never see O'Kane again.

THE NEWS MEDIA that accompanied Harold Stassen and his liberators included a *New York Times* reporter, Julius Ochs Adler. By coincidence, Adler's editor was from O'Kane's hometown in New Hampshire. When he discovered that O'Kane was among the liberated, the editor asked Adler to also wire his report from Japan directly to the O'Kane family.

Ernestine was overjoyed when she read the following wire story:

Aboard the *USS. Reeves*, in Tokyo Bay, August 30:

The saga of the submarine *Tang* and her nine survivors cannot be retold too often. It ranks among the epics of American naval history. In daring raids in Formosa Strait this little ship sank thirteen enemy ships, including one destroyer, totaling more than 100,000 tons, between October 10 and October 24, 1944. Commander Richard H. O'Kane . . . told quietly and without emotion today . . . about the last day of his daring craft.[20]

The story listed the names of all nine survivors.

At last, the waiting was over. Her husband had definitely survived captivity. She did not yet know that he was lying, hovering between life and death, on a hospital ship in Tokyo Bay.

PART FOUR

Back from the Deep

Ex communi periculo, fraternitas
(From common peril, brotherhood)

15

Back from the Deep

SEPTEMBER 2, 1945, TOKYO BAY—Vice Admiral Lockwood had waited a long time for this moment. During the dark days of 1942, when the Japanese had stormed across the Pacific, their formal surrender had seemed only a distant possibility. But now Lockwood was among the Allied victors, in the front line of the top brass aboard the battleship *Missouri* in Tokyo Bay, watching as a Japanese delegation walked to a spot assigned them on the main deck.

General Douglas MacArthur, flanked by Admirals Nimitz and Halsey, stepped to a microphone.

"It is my earnest hope—indeed the hope of all mankind—that from this solemn occasion a better world shall emerge out of the blood and carnage of the past," said MacArthur, "a world founded upon faith and understanding, a world dedicated to the dignity of man and fulfillment of his most cherished wish for freedom, tolerance, and justice. . . ."[1]

It was an exceptional speech, the best of MacArthur's career. The Japanese present were surprised by his magnanimity. One later wondered if their most senior military leaders would have behaved the same way. Only one of them, General Yoshijiro Umezu, had had sufficient honor—and face—to show up.

"And so my fellow countrymen," MacArthur concluded, "today I report to you that your sons and daughters have served you well and faithfully. . . . They are homeward bound. Take care of them."[2]

THAT SAME DAY, back in America, Ernestine O'Kane wrote to the families of the *Tang*'s lost crew:

> *You may be sure that there is a constant aching in my heart for each one of you. There are no people finer than you and I feel that I know each of you and my sorrow for you goes deep into my heart. Words are inadequate to tell you what a great part your loved one took in helping to bring the war to its end. I pray each of you may find peace of mind with His help.*[3]

AFTER THE SURRENDER CEREMONY, Vice Admiral Lockwood was anxious to see his men as they returned to their home base in Pearl Harbor. Larry Savadkin was among the first to arrive back. He had returned on a C-54, as had Clay Decker and several of the other men. Some had looked back through the open doors of

C-54s as they flew high above Tokyo. At least one had stood and urinated onto the ashes thousands of feet below.

Savadkin told Lockwood that O'Kane had been treated terribly. But, he added, his skipper had never cracked.[4] He had revealed no sensitive information and not a word about Ultra.

A few days later, Lockwood met with O'Kane himself, his "underwater ace of aces." O'Kane was a shadow of his former self, weighing just eighty-eight pounds. It was obvious that Stassen and his men had arrived just in time.

O'Kane told Lockwood he did not want to return to the States just yet. He wanted to stay in Pearl Harbor to recuperate a little. "He probably felt that his condition was too shocking for his family to see," explained Lockwood. "He was just skin and bones. His arms and legs looked no bigger than an ordinary man's wrists, his eyes were a bright yellow from jaundice (the result of rat-contaminated rice, I was told), and the dysentery from which he suffered would have killed him in a few more weeks."

O'Kane was in the worst shape of all, but plenty of others were pitifully thin and close to death. Lockwood was enraged by their treatment: "It made my blood boil to see this human wreckage returning from the prison camps of an alleged civilized nation, and to compare them with the fat, insolent-looking German and Japanese prisoners I had seen in the United States."[5]

BILL LEIBOLD WAS DELIGHTED to be on U.S. soil. He was not only back in Hawaii but also in the same hospital in Pearl Harbor as O'Kane and other *Tang* survivors. Unlike his skipper, he was able to walk around.

A few days after arriving at the hospital, Leibold was escorted to a car where he joined Hayes Trukke and Pete Narowanski. The three survivors were then driven to the submarine base in Honolulu, where they were welcomed by none other than Lockwood himself. Lockwood chatted with them and asked them about their experiences, showing genuine concern, and then awarded Narowanski a Silver Star and presented the others with a submarine combat pin. He also pinned a Purple Heart on Bill Leibold's chest.

Lockwood offered to put the men up at the Royal Hawaiian hotel. They were welcome to stay and "fatten up a little bit." But Leibold and his fellow survivors were eager to get home and declined Lockwood's offer.

Soon enough, they were on their way to the States. When they arrived, they were admitted to the Oak Knoll Naval Hospital in Oakland, California.[6] When Leibold was weighed, he discovered that he was down to one hundred pounds, seventy less than he had been on the *Tang*.

Dick O'Kane was the only one of the *Tang* survivors to stay on in Hawaii. Six weeks would pass before he was fit enough to be flown across America to the Naval Hospital in New Hampshire, where he would receive medical treatment for many more months before finally returning to duty in early 1946.

FLOYD CAVERLY stepped onto U.S. soil for the first time in almost two years in Alameda, across the bay from San Francisco. Like Bill Leibold, he also went to Oak Knoll Hospital. To his utter consternation, he was placed in a mental ward, the only place where there was a free bed. Caverly fumed—he had survived hell in Japan only to end up in a "nut ward."

Caverly searched the hospital and found a female nursing officer.

"Madam, I have been locked up for a year," said Caverly. "I'm not going to be locked up tonight. Open that damned gate and let me out of here."[7]

Eventually, Caverly was placed on a different ward. The following day, he tracked down his wife, Leone, who was teaching in a local dental nursing school. It was an intensely joyous reunion with her and their three-year-old daughter, Mary Anne. The last time he had seen Mary Anne, she had not even begun to walk.

Floyd and Leone had spent just a few months together in the five years since they had been married, and Caverly was determined to make up for lost time. "It didn't take me too damn long to get her pregnant," he recalled. "We just did what came naturally."[8]

Three days after Caverly returned to his home on Sunnydale Avenue in San Francisco, he received a check for a thousand dollars, his life insurance policy payout. He sent the check back with a note: "Try another year . . . I might be dead then but I'm not yet."[9]

BILL LEIBOLD'S WIFE, Grace, was working as a clerk in the public records office in Los Angeles that September. One morning, a reporter she knew from the *Los Angeles Times* spotted a teletype that listed a certain "William K. Leibold, Chief Boatswain's Mate" as being among the liberated Americans. The journalist had visited Grace's office several times and knew that her husband had gone missing with the *Tang*.[10] He quickly figured that William K. was in fact William R. Leibold and rushed over to the hall of records where Grace worked. Since receiving a telegram announcing that Leibold was presumed lost, she had heard nothing more of her husband's fate.

The reporter showed Grace the teletype. The man mentioned

had to be her husband.[11] Grace gasped. Could it be true? Then she bit her tongue, trying to hold back her tears.

"Golly, golly! But I never gave up hope that he was alive. I just couldn't feel he was dead."[12]

The journalist from the *Los Angeles Times* had a photographer with him. To this day, Bill Leibold cherishes the photograph he took of Grace, sitting behind a typewriter, wearing a pretty flowered dress, making the "A-okay" sign with one hand, grinning from ear to ear, her eyes sparkling with pure joy.

Grace and Bill were soon able to speak on the telephone. Grace was all for getting in a car and driving up to Oak Knoll Hospital to see her husband, but he discouraged her. He was in bad shape. Like Dick O'Kane, he wanted to regain some strength before seeing his wife again.

A few days later, Leibold arrived in Los Angeles and hailed a taxi that took him to his in-laws' house, where Grace was living. No one was home, so he sat on the stoop and waited. Suddenly, a familiar car pulled up. It was his old Ford coupe. Grace was driving it. Then his parents and his in-laws arrived in another car. "It was great to see her drive up in my car," he recalled. "What had kept guys like me going was the hope of that happening. She got out and there were lots of hugs and kisses. My parents were there too—all the family."[13]

ACROSS TOWN, another Los Angeles resident was just as happy as Bill Leibold's young wife and parents. His name was James B. DaSilva, father of Jesse DaSilva, and he too had just discovered that his son was alive.

When a reporter informed him that Jesse was on his way home, he appeared at first not to believe it. The reporter assured him that it was true. The sixty-year-old James DaSilva then fell silent, trying to control his feelings. His wife, Edith, had died three years ago, aged just forty-six, leaving him with two sons, Jesse and Jimmy, both of whom had joined the navy when war broke out. Then there had been that dreadful telegram, and the constant worry that Jimmy, too, would be lost along with Jesse—that his whole family would be dead by war's end.

But, then, James DaSilva's smile slowly returned.

"I was sure he'd come back," he said. "Now I know Jimmy will be alright, too."[14]

"FOR SOME OF US it was a long and trying voyage home," recalled Dick O'Kane. "But once there our recovery was complete. Best of all, our prayers had been answered and we found our families and loved ones fine."[15]

It was not so happy a homecoming for others among the survivors.

Clay Decker had returned on a C-54 plane, thanks to his famous cellmate, Pappy Boyington, who had arranged for Decker to be flown out of Yokosuka Naval Base in Japan, then to Guam, and then to the States. On the morning of September 7, at Alameda Naval Air Station, a crowd of tearful and overjoyed wives and relatives greeted Decker and twenty other men liberated from Japanese camps. The press was also waiting. A photographer snapped Decker holding his four-year-old son, Harry, who was dressed in a child's navy uniform, and hugging Lucille, his red-headed wife, as he kissed her on the cheek.[16]

Once they were in private, it wasn't long before Lucille broke the terrible news. As with so many of the wives of the *Tang*'s crew, she had assumed the worst when she had received the missing in action telegram. Since then, she had remarried.

Decker was stunned. "It was a great shock to both of us," he recalled. "She was shocked to find out that I was alive. I was shocked to find out that I was no longer Papa-san."[17]

Lucille had not only remarried, she had also collected on Decker's life insurance for almost six months.[18] The following months were a heartbreaking period, but Decker managed eventually to gain custody of Harry. "During the times when I was taking beatings," Decker recalled, "I would say to myself: 'Let them beat me. I can take this. I'm going to get back to where I see that little boy of mine.'"[19]

Decker and the other enlisted men soon received a dollar a day in back pay for the time they had been in prison camps in Japan. Decker cashed the check, bought a car, and drove with his son back to Colorado, where he had grown up.[20] It was tough starting over again, especially as a single parent, but the following year, 1946, he met and then married a woman named Ann, who would remain his wife for the rest of his life. Decker considered going back to college but instead went to work for an oil company so he could support his family. In the mid-sixties, he set up a successful garbage business which, by the time he sold it before retirement, had over forty employees.

Decker stayed in touch with the other *Tang* survivors and his cellmate in Ofuna, Pappy Boyington, who quickly descended into a vortex of failed marriages and alcoholism after his return to the States. Boyington had often lifted men's spirits in Omori by telling them he would hold a big party after the war on the top floor of a hotel in San Francisco. He was true to his word. Decker went to it and had a ball.

LARRY SAVADKIN RETURNED to find that his wife, Sarah, whom he had known for only a few months before marrying, had met and fallen in love with another man and given him a child. They were soon divorced.[21] Somehow, he retained his sense of humor and zest for life and remained remarkably unembittered by his experiences. He remarried in 1947 and opted to stay in the navy rather than finish a degree in engineering, explaining to his parents that he would qualify for a pension earlier with the navy and had "already learned more about engineering in the service" than he would ever learn at college.[22]

Jesse DaSilva, by contrast, wanted to return to civilian life. He left the navy and found a job in the Los Angeles area after the war. He soon met a young woman, Joyce, at the Lutheran church he had attended before joining the *Tang*. They were married in 1947 and went on to have three children, two daughters and a boy. "I always said that I married a man who came back from the dead," his wife would say years later. "When Jesse had gone missing, our minister in the church we were married in had asked the congregation to pray for his safe return."[23]

TO THEIR DYING DAYS, some prisoners of the Japanese continued to hate their captors with a startling intensity, exacerbated by the Japanese government's refusal to pay adequate compensation as Germany had.

Among the *Tang* survivors, there were mixed feelings. Some could forgive but none could forget. "Even when Larry first came back from Japan," recalled Savadkin's sister, Barbara, "he never talked about the horrors he had seen. He talked instead about the civilians who had given him food in Japan. Before the war, we had eaten potatoes and rice a great deal. He noticed that my mother no longer served rice at meals. He said he had no problem with rice. He said it was quite the opposite—'We never got enough rice. Please go back to rice.'"[24]

The last place on earth Bill Leibold wanted to visit after the war was Japan. "I didn't care for the Japanese," he recalled.[25] But during two visits to Japan after the war he came to realize that in every culture there is good and bad, the bestial and the humane. In 1947, he flew back, reluctantly, to testify in the war crimes trials that were underway in Tokyo. Years later, in 1960, he returned again to help set up a new Japanese navy—he even had a hand in the commissioning of Japan's first post-war submarine.

Dick O'Kane was also asked to testify at the war crimes trials. Larry Savadkin was the only other man from the *Tang* who returned to give testimony. He noted wryly that "most Japanese being tried or interrogated had very poor memories."[26]

Their fellow survivor Floyd Caverly did not go to Tokyo, although he was keen to do so. "I had some very good plans on how to wipe out some Japs while I was in prison camp," he later said. "That's why the old man wouldn't let me go to the war crimes trials. He was afraid I'd smuggle in a .45 and start shooting the hell out of them—Tojo and those bastards on trial. I could have broken his head in and stood around and laughed about it."[27]

16

To the Last Man

MARCH 27, 1946, WASHINGTON, D.C.—Dick O'Kane was standing tall and proud in the White House, in front of his family and old friend, Murray Frazee, when President Truman presented him with the Medal of Honor for his actions during the *Tang*'s fifth patrol.

Truman cited O'Kane's last two attacks before the *Tang* had sunk herself.[1]

"This is a saga of one of the greatest submarine cruisers of all time," concluded Truman, "led by her illustrious, gallant, and courageous commanding officer, and his crew of daring officers and men."[2]

O'Kane was now one of the most decorated Americans of the war—and the *Tang* arguably its most legendary submarine. The other survivors and some of the deceased from the *Tang* also received awards, which O'Kane had recommended. Fellow survivor Lieutenant Larry Savadkin and the *Tang's* executive officer, Lieutenant Frank Springer, who drowned in the conning tower, both received Navy Crosses. There were Silver Stars for survivors Floyd Caverly, Jesse DaSilva, Clay Decker, Hank Flanagan, Bill Leibold, Pete Narowanski, and Hayes Trukke, as well as for thirteen others who perished, including the young officer Mel Enos, John Heubeck, who was last seen swimming to China, Decker's best friend, George Zofcin, and Doc Larson, who had cared for his patients to the end.

For the success of her fourth and fifth patrols, the *Tang* received her second Presidential Unit Citation, becoming one of only three U.S. Navy vessels ever to receive that honor twice.

Dick O'Kane stayed in the navy, commanding the submarine supply ship USS *Pelias*. He was then appointed commander of the Submarine School in New London, before captaining another submarine supply ship, USS *Sperry*. A series of desk jobs in Washington followed, but he quickly became disillusioned and bored on land. He was a man of the sea, a hunter to the last. He had little patience for bureaucracy and did not like the way the navy was developing during the Cold War. "He disagreed with the navy about how they were preparing for a Third World War using Second World War technology," recalled Bill Leibold, who stayed in close touch with O'Kane.[3]

In July 1957, O'Kane resigned with the tombstone rank of rear admiral. None of his post-war assignments had come close to the thrill and satisfaction of captaining a submarine in wartime. Because his pension was just $358 per month, O'Kane worked for the Great Lakes Carbon Corporation in New York City until 1962, and then retired to a small horse ranch in the hills of Sonoma

County, north of San Francisco. He delighted in working on the ranch, where he often hosted old navy colleagues, including the *Tang*'s survivors, and wrote two best-selling books about his wartime experiences.

THE TOUGH IRISHMAN, Hank Flanagan, was the first of the survivors to die, in 1957, his early death no doubt hastened by his treatment as a POW. "One of the Japs had hit him on the head with a baseball bat," recalled Floyd Caverly. "It cracked his skull, and there was a tumor that started to form underneath, and the next thing he knew he was having severe headaches."[4]

Flanagan had divorced after returning from Japan. "He had told me he wasn't going to take orders from anyone anymore," recalled Bill Leibold. "[His] time as a POW affected him a great deal. He had a hard time when he came home."[5]

THERE WERE OTHER SAD ENDINGS. Shortly after the war, while still in the navy, Hayes Trukke helped pull a pilot from a crashed plane. An officer on duty at the time argued with Trukke, reprimanding him for not following regulations. In the heat of the argument, Trukke snapped and hit the officer, knocking him out. Commended for saving the pilot, he was also hauled on the carpet for striking a superior. He soon left the navy and joined the Los Angeles Police Department.

Trukke had been badly affected by the countless beatings he had received as a prisoner of war, and he apparently drank heavily after retiring to Flagstaff, Arizona, where he had grown up. According to a fellow submarine veteran, Bill Gallagher, Trukke died in 1981 a broken-hearted, embittered man. "His true love married while he was a prisoner," Gallagher wrote Jesse DaSilva. "He later married, had one son, whom he lost at age five. He then turned to alcohol."[6]

The exact circumstances of his death were a mystery, but alcoholism was thought to be a factor. "We heard that he had died in a swimming accident," recalled Bill Leibold. "He was a strong swimmer, so some of us wondered what had really happened. Some say he was drunk and fell into the swimming pool and drowned."[7]

Trukke had left an important legacy. He proved that a man could free float from a submerged submarine and live to tell the tale. In the late 1940s, the British navy had sent over submarine officers to question Trukke at length. In a subsequent report, they recommended that all British submarines adopt the "blow and go" technique, which Trukke had used to save his life, as standard escape practice.[8]

THE *Tang* survivors stuck together as they aged. At one reunion, Pete Narowanksi disappeared into a bedroom at a hotel only to reemerge wearing the same brightly-colored trunks he had worn so long ago in the water when the *Tang* had gone down. Incredibly, he had managed to keep them from falling to shreds during his time as a POW.[9]

Floyd Caverly recalled other reunions in the eighties attended by his skipper. He had noticed that O'Kane's essential personality was unchanged although he was dealing with the onset of Alzheimer's. To his crew, he was still an undersea hunter. Caverly remembered one reunion when O'Kane, even as a gaunt, old man, went down on one knee, pretending to take bearings and ranges, still telling his crew: "Hold me up now. Don't dip me." He was still the old O'Kane. "He knew every damn ship we ever sunk," recalled Caverly. "He'd tell you where it was sunk, the name. He remembered every detail."[10]

IN 1985, two days before Valentine's Day, Dick O'Kane received a telephone call at his ranch.

"Admiral O'Kane?" asked an unfamiliar voice.

O'Kane identified himself.

"I have found your ring," said Navy Pharmacist's Mate Wayne Schutts.

O'Kane was amazed. Schutts had found the diamond and sapphire encrusted engagement ring he had given Ernestine on Valentine's Day 1936. It had been lost while the couple had been surfing on Oahu in the late thirties. Schutts explained that he had found the ring, engraved with "RHOK," under a foot of sand off Oahu beach, with the help of a metal detector.

O'Kane paid for Schutts to fly to his ranch in California and hand deliver the ring so that he and Ernestine could personally thank him.[11]

In letters to family, friends, and inquisitive reporters and historians, right to the end of his life, O'Kane stressed how much he still loved Ernestine, often ending correspondence with the number of years they had been married. It was the thought of Ernestine that had kept him alive in the water and through the POW camps all those years ago, and Ernestine herself who had helped him through the long and painful rehabilitation after he had come home a physical wreck.

ONE AFTERNOON on his beloved Red Hill Horse Ranch in California, O'Kane was walking with Bill Leibold, who had become an ever closer friend as the years passed.

O'Kane still ribbed Leibold about the moment when he had nearly dislocated O'Kane's shoulder, trying to attract his attention to the Japanese destroyer that was bearing down on them. He deeply respected Leibold, who had remained in the navy, becoming a highly regarded diving expert specializing in submarine rescue, and forming the first Navy Seal teams while on assignment to Washington in 1960. Leibold had eventually captained his own ship, the USS *Volodar*, and had risen to the rank of commander before retiring with his wife, Grace, to a beautiful home on top of Mount Palomar, north of San Diego.

That afternoon on the ranch, O'Kane surprised Leibold.

"Do you remember Ofuna?" O'Kane asked.

Leibold nodded.

"You can never forget," said O'Kane.[12]

In his last years, sadly, Dick O'Kane did start to forget—he suffered Alzheimer's to the point where he could no longer recognize Leibold when he visited.

A FORTNIGHT AFTER his eighty-third birthday, on February 16, 1994, Dick O'Kane died of pneumonia. He was buried at Arlington National Cemetery, the most decorated submarine officer of World War II.

Four years after O'Kane's death, a new destroyer was named after him. At the launching of the USS *O'Kane* in Maine, in March 1998, two survivors were present for the ceremony, Bill Leibold and Floyd Caverly, and of course, O'Kane's "childhood chum"— his widow, eighty-five-year-old Ernestine O'Kane, designated the ship's matron of honor. They watched with great pride as O'Kane's granddaughter, thirty-six-year-old Leslie Allen Berry, smashed a red, white, and blue bottle of champagne on a metal hull. Then the Aegis-guided missile destroyer slid down ways into the Kennebec River at the Bath Iron Works shipyard. As a boy, O'Kane had sailed the very same river.

At the dedication ceremony, Congressman Tom Allen addressed a sizable crowd.

"Today," said Allen, "we have devalued terms like 'hero' and 'courage,' applying them loosely to athletes with multimillion dollar contracts and movie stars whose feats are no more than celluloid fantasies. The destroyer we launch today [celebrates] a genuine hero from an age when heroism truly meant something."[13]

When interviewed by the local press, Ernestine said her husband had rarely talked with her about the war. In her eyes, he had been a homebody, a great cook. He had not had "much interest" in the medals and other honors showered upon him.

Then, she added, reflectively, "The hardest thing for him the rest of his life was that he came home and his men didn't."[14]

In the newspaper report describing the launching, it was pointed out that O'Kane's first submarine "was sunk four months after O'Kane left to become executive officer of the USS *Wahoo*. That vessel, too, was sunk after O'Kane left."[15] It was only his last submarine, the *Tang*, that had sunk with him still on board.

All his adult life, O'Kane was honored for his bravery. Over and over, it was pointed out that, in Mush Morton's words, he had been "the bravest man."[16] That may have been true. But as far as O'Kane had been concerned, he had simply made fewer errors than others. "There's no margin for mistakes in submarines," he had told the *Tang*'s crew over and over. "You're either dead or alive."[17]

PETE NAROWANSKI DIED the same day as Dick O'Kane, of a heart attack in his sleep. "That's the way it was with Pete," observed Clay Decker. "Wherever the commander went, he followed."[18]

Narowanski's daughter, Jackie, recalled that her father had been hurt deep inside and permanently changed by what had happened to him in Ofuna: "Sometimes he would take me for a drive when I was a small kid and say nothing for hours on end. He never talked about what had happened in the war until he went to one of the last reunions of the *Tang* survivors in the early nineties. He then told me he could still remember the sound of rats scurrying around when he had been tied up and blindfolded in a wooden shack."[19]

After the war, Narowanski had become something of a loner. He had married a Russian woman in the late 1940s, mostly to please his mother, but the marriage lasted less than a year. A chronic gambler, Narowanski then took to "playing the horses all the time," recalled Floyd Caverly. "He used to go up and down the East Coast, following the horses. He found a horse and if it made a little money for him he would follow it up and down. Anytime his horse moved, well Old Pete went with him."[20] On a clear afternoon in 1988, he finally hit the big time. The track was fast and the odds very long, but Pete Narowanski was in luck. He went home that evening with thirty-four thousand dollars in his pocket, having won a Trifecta.[21]

Narowanski loved to swim and hunt well into old age. "He grew up in the water," recalled his daughter. "He was always an avid swimmer. He was still muscular, still in great shape, when he died—the same day his captain passed away."[22]

Jackie was still close to her father when he died. She knew that his wartime experiences, and the friendships he had formed with his fellow *Tang* survivors, were the most important of his life. "At the last reunion my father attended, I went along to meet the other men. They were lively, happy, and still glad they had gotten to come home."

CLAY DECKER AND JESSE DASILVA increasingly lived in the past as they got closer to death. Among the nine survivors, they were the most active in veterans' organizations, perhaps because they had left the navy soon after the war and had all the more reason, and time, to become nostalgic. DaSilva eventually became president of the National Association of U.S. Submarine Veterans of World War II.

On a return visit to Pearl Harbor late in life, he went aboard the USS *Bowfin* in Honolulu. "Seeing that boat brought back a lot of old memories," he said before adding that it was a miracle that he survived the *Tang*'s sinking and then Japanese imprisonment.

DaSilva had worked as a pressman at the *Los Angeles Times* from 1946 until retirement.[23] He was the only one of the *Tang* survivors who wanted to return to the Formosa Strait to find out what had happened to the *Tang*. "I have a desire to go back and dive down and see exactly where we were hit," DaSilva said in 1992. "I would not want to disturb anything. I'd like to place a wreath in honor of the men who are still there, put it over the sheers. The *Tang* should be treated like the *Arizona*."[24]

DaSilva asked himself many times why he had survived when others had not. "Why me? I haven't come up with an answer. Why was I saved? I was saved for a purpose but I have not put my finger on it. I don't think I ever will."[25]

DaSilva thought he might have found out why by the time he was diagnosed with terminal cancer in 1998. He had perhaps been spared so he could pass on the story of the *Tang* and her crew to others, in particular to relatives of the men who didn't come back. To that end, he managed to track down the son of Glen Haws, his best friend on the *Tang*. Buck Haws had been born during the *Tang's* final patrol. He had never even been held by his father. DaSilva was able to tell him all he could.[26]

DaSilva's daughter, Joyce Paul, was with him at the end when he died of lymphoma. "While my father had a very painful last five months of his life while the lymphoma was killing him," she recalled, "I saw God work in wonderful ways, allowing my father to ask forgiveness where needed and say good-bye to his many friends." The visit to Haws's son, she believed, had resolved any feelings of survivor's guilt.[27]

In 2000, two years after DaSilva died, the *Kursk*, the Russian nuclear submarine, sank in the Barents Sea. The world's press suddenly went looking for anyone who had escaped from a sunken submarine. Only one man was still alive of those who had done so from the *Tang*. "I know what's going through those boys' minds," seventy-nine-year-old Clay Decker told *USA Today*. "We knew when we went aboard the submarine that we might end up with this iron cylinder being our tomb."[28]

Not one of the *Kursk's* 116 sailors survived.

Before he died in 2003, Clay Decker said that the war often felt as if it had been a dream. But every so often it would all come surging back.[29] For many years, like most of the other *Tang* men, he had struggled with post-traumatic stress, waking up some nights in a cold sweat. The experience would last only a few minutes, but the memory of escaping from the deep had become, if anything, more and more vivid as the years passed.

THE PAST ALSO HAUNTED Larry Savadkin to the end. Although he had survived the sinking of two vessels, he continued his career in the navy, going on to command his own submarine, the SS-302, *Sabalo*. In early 1953, he and his crew encountered a fierce typhoon in the Sea of Japan, reminiscent of the one the *Tang* had endured on her final patrol. Under Savadkin's command, the *Sabalo* rode out the storm and then docked in Yokosuka in Japan. The visit bought back vivid memories.

Savadkin reminisced about the *Tang* with Lieutenant Robert Bell, the *Sabalo*'s engineering and diving officer, joking with him that the *Tang* had made her "fastest dive" after she had been struck by her own torpedo.

While in Yokosuka, Savadkin left the ship to see if he could find Ofuna. Lieutenant Bell remembered how Savadkin located the camp, despite the fact that the prisoners had always been blindfolded when they went out the gates. "He orientated himself by the position of the huge electrical power cables," recalled Bell. "Using the same technique, he found the general area, but the Japanese had rotated the buildings and changed the streets. They did this probably out of shame and fear. Nevertheless, Larry found where he had been and proved it by tearing up the floorboards and finding a Red Cross package he had hidden years before to keep the guards from stealing it."[30]

Savadkin was not tied to submarines, and after the *Sabalo* served on the carrier USS *Valley Forge*. He then worked as an officer in the Unconventional War Department and held high-level advisory positions in Istanbul and Belgium. He retired in 1972 and spent the last years of his life in an elegant home overlooking a golf course in San Marcos, California. Like O'Kane, he suffered from Alzheimer's before he died in 2007.

Before Savadkin died, his younger sister, Barbara, wondered why he was sometimes in such mental distress. After talking with Bill Leibold, she realized that her brother was experiencing flashbacks to his time as a prisoner of war, when he had been beaten so often and without warning, often until he lost count of the blows.[31]

FLOYD CAVERLY HAD ALSO STAYED in the navy after the war. He said nothing about his injured back, afraid he would not be let back into the submarine service. "Two vertebrae had been cracked and grown back together badly," he recalled. "The pain was terrible."[32] Caverly finally retired from the navy after he was asked to go on a carrier: "I had been in the submarine service and didn't want to go. . . . So I said 'No. I have my twenty [years] in, so I'm going to quit.'"[33]

In 2008, aged ninety, Floyd Caverly lived with his second wife in a small town in central Oregon, delighting in his great-grandchildren and still in regular contact with Bill Leibold, the only other living survivor from the *Tang*. He had lost none of the sharp humor that had made him so popular on the *Tang*.

Caverly still had nightmares about his time in Japan. He could still vividly recall the beatings he suffered, which had caused him daily pain for sixty-two years. "They would start beating your back, or your ribs if you were sleeping on your back. They'd hit you right across the stomach, or across the pelvis with that damn club. This was funny to them. You'd hear them laughing and giggling and telling one another about it."[34]

At age eighty-five, when asked to look back on his many years in the navy, Bill Leibold was just as proud as his last surviving crewmate, Floyd Caverly, of his time on the *Tang*. It seemed somehow fitting that these two men were still able to argue and joke about who actually kept who alive that night long ago in October 1944.

Both were modest, reticent men—and submariners to their core. They were not the kind to make grandiose statements or dwell on the broader significance of their roles aboard World War II's greatest American submarine. Among the few survivors of a unique breed of naval warrior, they had belonged to the American navy's last corsairs, men whose antecedents had defeated the British in hit-and-run raids, stealing away at dead of night or under a smoke screen.

THE LAST TWO SURVIVORS of the *Tang* remained in close contact. Bill Leibold also stayed in touch with the O'Kane family, particularly with Ernestine and her daughter Marsha. When Ernestine became too frail to talk on the telephone, Leibold began to check up on her through Marsha. He had known Marsha practically all her life, since she was just five years old and had stood on the bridge of the *Tang* during a trial run in 1943 and stared at the Golden Gate Bridge passing above her. Several reunions, countless phone calls over the years, and ever more poignant memories had created a powerful bond.

To this day, Marsha remains convinced that Leibold and her father had a pact as prisoners: whoever survived would take care of the other's family. She knows this must be true because she nursed her father in his last years, often walking with him along a local beach that he loved, talking with him about the past, about his time as a prisoner and his great affection for "Boats," as he still called Leibold.

As a child, Marsha had watched her father fly-fish in the Tuolumne Meadows in Yosemite. After the war, when she was a teenager, he had taught her to swim every stroke expertly. He had even made her practice staying afloat in the cold waters of the Merced River in California so that she would be able to survive, just as he had, if she found herself in a similar situation.

Eventually, father and daughter could no longer go near rivers or the ocean together. As he lost his final battle—against Alzheimer's—the mere sight of water would transport him back to that terrible night in 1944 when he had survived, unlike so many of his men. "To the very end, my father suffered tremendous survivor's guilt," Marsha recalled in 2007. "He talked to me about it a lot. He felt that he had not lived up to the naval creed. He had not gone down with his boat."

For some reason, the sound of foghorns brought the past flooding back with particularly traumatic force. Then O'Kane would grab his daughter by the arm and start to pull her toward the ocean.

"We have to go," O'Kane would say. "We have to go. . . . We have to go save them."[35]

SURVIVORS OF THE USS *TANG*

Commander Richard H. O'Kane, Commanding Officer
Lt. Commander Lawrence Savadkin, Engineering Officer
Lieutenant (jg) Henry J. Flanagan, Torpedo Officer
Radio Technician Floyd Caverly
Chief Boatswain's Mate William Leibold
Motor Machinist's Mate Jesse DaSilva
Motor Machinist's Mate Clayton Decker
Torpedoman's Mate Hayes Trukke
Torpedoman's Mate Pete Narowanski

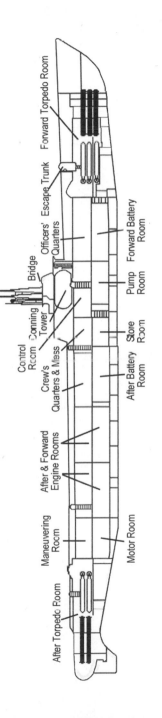

USS *Tang*

Forward Torpedo Room

Officers' Escape Trunk

Officers' Quarters

Bridge

Control Room

Conning Tower

Crew's Quarters & Mess

After & Forward Engine Rooms

Maneuvering Room

After Torpedo Room

Forward Battery Room

Pump Room

Store Room

After Battery Room

Motor Room

NOTES

Chapter 1

1. Daniel Ford, "Audacity and Heroism, Underwater," *Wall Street Journal*, December 31, 2001.

2. Floyd Caverly, interview with the author.

3. Ibid.

4. William Tuohy, *The Bravest Man: The Story of Richard O'Kane & U.S. Submariners in the Pacific War* (Stroud, England: Sutton Publishing, 2001), p. 282.

5. William Leibold, interview with the author.

6. http://www.lafayette.edu/news.php/viewnc/40-print.

7. Edward L. Beach, *Submarine!* (Annapolis, Maryland: Blue-jacket Books, 2003), p. 164.

8. Ibid.

9. Ibid.

10. Caverly.

11. Beach, p. 164.

12. Dick O'Kane, quoted in James F. DeRose, *Unrestricted Warfare: How a New Breed of Officers Led the Submarine Force to Victory in World War II* (New York: John Wiley & Sons, 2000), p. 192.

13. Clay Decker, oral history, Regis University.

14. Ibid.

15. Ibid.

16. Ibid.

17. Beach, p. 166.

18. Ibid.

19. Ibid.

20. Richard O'Kane, *Clear the Bridge! The War Patrols of the U.S.S. Tang* (New York: Ballantine Books, 1977), pp. 320–321.

21. Decker.

22. Murray Frazee, "We Never Looked Back" (*Navy Times,* July 1994).

23. Frazee, unpublished autobiography, p. 54.

24. Frazee, "We Never Looked Back."

25. Frazee, unpublished autobiography, p. 53.

26. Frazee, interview with the author.

27. Leibold, letter to the author.

28. Caverly.

Chapter 2

1. Clay Decker, oral history, Regis University.

2. The *Tang* was the first boat in the U.S. Navy to be named after a surgeonfish.

3. Decker.

4. Floyd Caverly, interview with the author.

5. Richard O'Kane, *Clear the Bridge!* (New York: Ballantine Books, 1977), p. 375.

6. Murray Frazee, unpublished autobiography, pp. 51–52.

7. Marsha O. Allen, interview with the author.

8. More than one in ten of his graduating class would be lost during the war.

9. William Leibold, interview with the author.

10. Caverly.

11. Leibold, interview with the author.

12. Ibid.

13. William Tuohy, *The Bravest Man* (Stroud, England: Sutton Publishing, 2001), p. 166.

14. O'Kane, p. 472.

15. Tuohy, p. 167.

16. *Lookout* (June 19, 2006, Vol. 51, No. 25).

17. Ibid.

18. Tuohy, pp. 172–174.

19. Chief Boatswain's Mate Bill Leibold was another of the crew who had been surprised by just how far O'Kane was willing to go in readying the *Tang* and her crew for war. Leibold, letter to the author.

20. Murray Frazee, interview with the author.

21. Leibold, interview with the author.

22. Edward L. Beach, *Submarine!* (Annapolis, Maryland: Bluejacket Books, 2003), pp. 170–171.

23. O'Kane, pp. 372–373.

24. O'Kane was always trying to minimize the time needed for a refit. Murray Frazee, unpublished autobiography, p. 53.

25. Caverly.

26. Tuohy, p. 305.

Chapter 3

1. Richard O'Kane, *Clear the Bridge!* (New York: Ballantine Books, 1977), p. 373.

2. Ibid.

3. Ibid. pp. 373–374.

4. In another incident, Chief Quartermaster Sidney Jones had almost thrown Walker overboard because he looked as if he had

fallen asleep during a watch. Floyd Caverly, interview with the author.

5. Ibid.

6. O'Kane, pp. 376–377.

7. J. T. MacDaniel, ed., *USS* Tang *(SS-306) American Submarine War Patrol Reports* (Georgia: Riverdale Books, 2005), p. 132.

8. It had taken just six hours after the Japanese attack for all American naval commanders to be ordered to "execute unrestricted air and submarine warfare against Japan."

9. O'Kane, pp. 376–377.

10. Clay Decker, oral history, Regis University.

11. Caverly.

12. O'Kane, p. 380.

13. Chris Stout, letter to the author.

14. MacDaniel, p. 132.

15. Murray Frazee, "We Never Looked Back" (*Navy Times*, July 1994).

16. MacDaniel, p. 132.

17. Hervie Haufler, *Codebreakers' Victory* (New York: New American Library, 2003), p. 219.

18. MacDaniel, p. 133.

19. Caverly.

20. O'Kane, p. 383.

21. Caverly.

22. William Tuohy, *The Bravest Man* (Stroud, England: Sutton Publishing, 2001), 2001, p. 308.

23. O'Kane, p. 385.

24. Ibid.

25. Ibid.

26. William Leibold, interview with the author.

27. O'Kane, p. 386.

28. Ibid.

29. Leibold.

30. Ibid.

31. Allowing the *Tang* to be buffeted along by the storm was out of the question. The storm could last for days, well beyond the reserves of battery power.

32. O'Kane, p. 388.

33. Caverly.

34. O'Kane, p. 389.

35. All the torpedoes hit their targets.

36. Cindy Adams, "USS *Tang* Survivors" (*Polaris*, February 1981).

Chapter 4

1. J. T. MacDaniel, ed., *USS* Tang *(SS-306) American Submarine War Patrol Reports* (Georgia: Riverdale Books, 2005), p. 133.

2. William Tuohy, *The Bravest Man* (Stroud, England: Sutton Publishing, 2001), p. 244.

3. Floyd Caverly, interview with the author.

4. William Leibold, letter to the author.

5. Clay Decker, oral history, Regis University.

6. MacDaniel, p. 133.

7. Edward L. Beach, *Submarine!* (Annapolis, Maryland: Bluejacket Books, 2003), p. 154.

8. Robin Enos, letter to the author.

9. MacDaniel, p. 134.

10. Ibid.

11. Leibold, interview with the author.

12. Tuohy, p. 312.

13. Richard O'Kane, *Clear the Bridge!* (New York: Ballantine Books, 1977), p. 406.

14. Murray Frazee, unpublished autobiography, p. 53.

15. George Grider, *Warfish* (New York: Little Brown, 1958), p. 56.

16. Ibid., p. 57.

17. Ibid.

18. Ibid., p. 62.

19. Clay Blair, *Silent Victory* (Annapolis, Maryland: Naval Institute Press, 2001), p. 383.

20. It was a failure that had left many captains such as Morton deeply embittered and had caused a grave crisis in the navy that was resolved only when Vice Admiral Lockwood campaigned relentlessly for proper testing. Finally, after thousands of lives had been risked only to see torpedoes fail to explode, continual problems with dud and faulty torpedoes and their exploders were overcome when Lockwood forced the introduction of new, lightweight firing pins for Mark 14 torpedoes set to explode on impact.

21. Blair, p. 384.

22. Grider, p. 73.

23. Blair, p. 384.

24. James F. DeRose, *Unrestricted Warfare* (New York: John Wiley & Sons, 2000), p. 84.

25. Ibid.

26. Grider, p. 73.

27. Ibid.

28. Beach, p. 152.

29. Ibid.

Chapter 5

1. Richard O'Kane, *Clear the Bridge!* (New York: Ballantine Books, 1977), p. 433.

2. William Tuohy, *The Bravest Man* (Stroud, England: Sutton Publishing, 2001), p. 315.

3. William Leibold, letter to the author.

4. Charles A. Lockwood, *Sink 'em All* (New York: Bantam Books, 1984), p. 218.

5. Leibold, interview with the author.

6. Edward L. Beach, *Submarine!* (Annapolis, Maryland: Bluejacket Books, 2003), p. 174.

7. Floyd Caverly, interview with the author.

8. Beach, p. 175.

9. James F. DeRose, *Unrestricted Warfare* (New York: John Wiley & Sons, 2000), p. 209.

10. Beach, p. 175.

11. Caverly, interview with the author.

12. Caverly, oral history, University of Minnesota.

13. Lockwood, p. 220.

14. Tuohy, p. 318.

15. Lockwood, p. 220.

16. DeRose, p. 212.

17. Leibold, interview with the author.

18. Torpedo 24 broached as soon as it left the *Tang*. DeRose, p. 212.

19. Leibold, interview with the author.

20. Jesse DaSilva, interview with Douglas E. Clanin. Indiana Historical Society.

21. Beach, p. 178.

22. Floyd Caverly, oral history, University of Minnesota.

23. O'Kane, p. 456.

24. Leibold, interview with the author.

25. O'Kane, p. 456.

Chapter 6

1. Floyd Caverly, interview with the author.

2. Caverly, oral history, University of Minnesota.

3. Ibid.

4. Cindy Adams, "USS *Tang* Survivors" (*Polaris*, February 1981).

5. "Loss of the U.S.S. *Tang*" (ComSubPac report, 1946), p. 252.

6. This was not always the case. A crewmember and an officer had to be restrained during a depth-charging on *Tang*'s first patrol; both had been quickly disqualified for submarine duty. William Leibold, letter to the author.

7. "Loss of the U.S.S. *Tang*," p. 252.

8. Ibid.

9. Leibold, interview with the author.

10. Caverly, interview with the author.

11. Caverly, oral history, University of Minnesota.

12. Caverly, interview with the author.

13. Caverly, oral history, University of Minnesota.

14. Leibold, interview with the author.

15. Ibid.

16. Caverly, interview with the author.

17. Ibid.

18. Ibid.

19. Ibid.

20. Richard O'Kane, *Clear the Bridge!* (New York: Ballantine Books, 2003), p. 456.

21. *Wall Street Journal*, December 31, 2001.

22. Leibold, interview with the author.

23. Ibid.

24. Ibid.

25. "Submarine Personnel and Depth Charges" (ComSubPac report, 1946), p. 185.

26. Ibid.

27. Caverly, oral history, University of Minnesota.

28. Ibid.

29. Ibid.

30. Caverly, interview with the author.

31. *Wall Street Journal*, December 31, 2001.

32. Marsha Allen, interview with the author.

33. "Loss of the U.S.S. *Tang*," p. 251.

34. Larry Savadkin, interview with the author.

35. Barbara Lane, interview with the author.

36. Ibid.

37. "Loss of the U.S.S. *Tang*," p. 251.

38. William Tuohy, *The Bravest Man* (Stroud, England: Sutton Publishing, 2001), p. 323.

39. "Loss of the U.S.S. *Tang*," p. 251.

40. Experiments have shown that the "break point" comes at 87 seconds. But if a person hyperventilates first, getting rid of carbon dioxide, it can come as late as 140 seconds.

41. Savadkin.

42. James F. DeRose, *Unrestricted Warfare* (New York: John Wiley & Sons, 2000), p. 216.

43. "Loss of the U.S.S. *Tang*," p. 252.

Chapter 7

1. "Loss of the U.S.S. Tang" (ComSubPac report, 1946), p. 252.

2. Clay Decker, oral history, Regis University.

3. Flint Whitlock, "Tragedy Aboard the *Tang*" (*WWII History*, March 2005).

4. Decker, oral history, Regis University.

5. "Trapped at Thirty Fathoms," Jesse DaSilva's story, as told to Bill Hagendorn, Indiana Historical Society.

6. Cindy Adams, *"USS* Tang *Survivors"* (*Polaris,* February 1981).

7. Edward L. Beach, *Submarine!* (Annapolis, Maryland: Bluejacket Books, 2003), p. 178.

8. DaSilva's story, as told to Bill Hagendorn.

9. Adams.

10. Ibid.

11. DaSilva's story, as told to Bill Hagendorn.

12. Ibid.

13. Beach, p. 180.

14. DaSilva's story, as told to Bill Hagendorn.

15. Adams.

16. James F. DeRose, *Unrestricted Warfare* (New York: John Wiley & Sons, 2000), p. 218.

17. DaSilva's story, as told to Bill Hagendorn.

18. Adams.

19. Adams.

20. The S-48 was soon considered the worst and most unlucky submarine in the U.S. Navy. Within months, one of her young lieutenants, Hyman George Rickover, the S-48's engineering officer, would selflessly go below and extinguish a serious battery fire. On January 29, 1935, the boat was again in trouble, running aground off Portsmouth, New Hampshire. She would remain in service, after being refloated, throughout World War II, acting as a training boat. Rickover would eventually become an admiral, most famously responsible for the U.S.'s first nuclear powered submarine.

21. "Loss of the U.S.S. *Tang*," p. 253.

22. Decker, oral history, Regis University.

23. Adams.

24. "Loss of the U.S.S. *Tang*," p. 252.

25. Ibid., p. 251.

26. Floyd Caverly, interview with the author.

27. DeRose, p. 219.

28. Adams.

29. Whitlock.

30. "Loss of the U.S.S. *Tang*," p. 253.

31. Ibid.

32. Ibid.

33. Ibid.

34. Adams.

35. "Loss of the U.S.S. *Tang*," p. 255.

36. Decker, oral history, Regis University.

37. Ibid.

38. DeRose, p. 218.

39. "Loss of the U.S.S. *Tang*," p. 255.

40. Ibid., p. 253.

41. Charles Bowers "Swede" Momsen had been thrown out of the United States Naval Academy in his first year for bad results. He persisted and graduated a year early. In 1923, he took command of his first submarine, the 0-15 (SS-76), and was then given command of S-1, the latest design of submarine in the U.S. Navy. On September 25, 1925, another submarine, the S-51, hit a cargo ship and sank in 130 feet of water. Momsen was ordered to search for the downed boat. He found an oil slick but could not locate the submarine. Momsen felt helpless. Later he became determined to find a way to help men escape from a submarine and be

rescued. The result was the Momsen Lung and an escape trunk used to rescue men from the *Squalus* in 1939.

42. The first recorded escape from a submerged submarine occurred in 1851 when the German submarine *Brandtraucher* plunged to the bottom in just sixty feet of water. Her captain, Wilhelm Bauer, who had designed the boat, stayed remarkably calm, assuring two other men aboard that if they waited for sufficient water to pour into the boat, the external and internal pressure would equalize and then they would be able to open a hatch and rise to the surface. This is exactly what happened. "We came to the surface like bubbles in a glass of champagne," Bauer recalled. The earliest American submarines, the first of which was commissioned by the U.S. government in 1895, were intended to operate in shallow coastal waters where Bauer's escape procedure could be repeated. Over the next century, enormous time, effort, and expense were directed at finding other ways to escape from a submarine, and yet none was as simple or effective at depths below three hundred feet as the method demonstrated by Bauer, much later dubbed "blow and go." Nevertheless, navies became slaves to technology, blinding many to the most basic method that Bauer had pioneered. Indeed, as submarines developed, so too did the quest for an artificial breathing device when none was arguably required.

43. Nine months later, after Herculean efforts, the U.S. Navy finally managed to raise the submarine.

44. DeRose, p. 219.

45. "Loss of the U.S.S. *Tang*," p. 255.

46. Ibid., p. 253.

47. Some of the men had not been trained in escape procedures. There had been precious little time to train them properly given the need to provide crews for the Silent Service. Some had

practiced escapes in the towers at New London and in San Diego, rising in controlled circumstances with divers close by to help them. But what they were about to attempt was altogether different. In fact it had never been attempted before.

48. Ann Jensen, "Why the Best Technology for Escaping from a Submarine Is No Technology" (*Invention & Technology Magazine*, Summer 1986).

49. Decker, oral history, Regis University.

50. Pete Narowanski later stated, "The system of tapping on the bulkhead gave our position to the enemy." "Loss of the U.S.S. *Tang*," p. 256.

51. Ibid.

52. Caverly.

53. Ibid.

54. Ibid.

55. "Loss of the U.S.S. *Tang*," p. 252.

56. Ibid.

57. Ibid., p.254

58. Caverly.

59. "Loss of the U.S.S. *Tang*," p. 256.

60. DeRose, p. 220.

Chapter 8

1. William Leibold, e-mail to the author.

2. Ibid.

3. Floyd Caverly, interview with the author.

4. Ibid.

5. Leibold, interview with the author.

6. "Loss of the U.S.S. *Tang*" (ComSubPac report, 1946), p. 253.

7. Clay Decker, oral history, Regis University.

8. "Loss of the U.S.S. *Tang*" (ComSubPac report, 1946), p. 258.

9. Decker.

10. William Tuohy, *The Bravest Man* (Stroud, England: Sutton Publishing, 2001), p. 329.

11. Decker.

12. Ibid.

13. Tom Burgess, "First Man Up, Last Man Out" (*Historical Diver*, Spring 2002).

14. Leibold, interview with the author.

15. Flint Whitlock, "Tragedy Aboard the *Tang*" (*WWII History*, March 2005).

16. Decker.

17. Ibid.

18. Ibid.

19. DeRose, p. 221.

20. Whitlock.

21. Decker.

Chapter 9

1. Pierce was thought to be one of the few men aboard who had actually practiced an escape from one hundred feet at the New London submarine school. "Loss of the U.S.S. *Tang*" (ComSubPac report, 1946), p. 254.

2. Ibid., p. 255.

3. Ibid., p. 256.

4. Ibid.

5. Ibid., p. 255.

6. Ibid.

7. James F. DeRose, *Unrestricted Warfare* (New York: John Wiley & Sons, 2000), p. 222.

8. Richard O'Kane, *Clear the Bridge!* (New York: Ballantine Books, 1977), p. 458.

9. The survivors from the forward torpedo room, as well as O'Kane and Savadkin, all agreed that death from asphyxiation was certain if the men weren't killed by an explosion caused by the fire in the battery compartment first. "Loss of the U.S.S. *Tang*," p. 256.

10. DeRose, p. 222.

11. William Leibold, interview with the author.

12. Ibid.

13. Tom Burgess, "First Man Up, Last Man Out" (*Historical Diver* Spring 2002).

14. "Loss of the U.S.S. *Tang*," p. 254.

15. Ibid.

16. "Loss of the U.S.S. *Tang*," p. 252.

17. Clay Decker, oral history, Regis University.

18. Cindy Adams, "USS *Tang* Survivors" (*Polaris*, February 1981).

19. Jackie Morris, interview with the author.

20. Ibid.

21. DeRose, p. 223.

22. Ibid.

23. "This Month" (Los Angeles: Pacific Southwest District of the Lutheran Church, February 1994).

24. Joyce Paul, interview with the author.

25. Paul, e-mail to the author.

26. DeRose, p. 223.

27. Jesse DaSilva, interview with Douglas E. Clanin.

28. DeRose, p. 223.

29. DaSilva, interview with Douglas E. Clanin.

30. Ibid.

31. "Loss of the U.S.S. *Tang*," p. 256.

32. "Trapped at Thirty Fathoms," Jesse DaSilva's story, as told to Bill Hagendorn, Indiana Historical Society.

33. Adams.

34. DaSilva's story, as told to Bill Hagendorn.

35. DaSilva, interview with Douglas E. Clanin.

36. Morris.

37. Floyd Caverly, interview with the author.

38. "Loss of the U.S.S. *Tang*," p. 254.

39. DaSilva, interview with Douglas E. Clanin.

40. Decker.

41. This was all the more remarkable in light of the fact that a later study figured that 94 percent of men known to be alive when submarines were disabled in WWII died inside them as they sank or rose to the surface. Ann Jensen, "Why the Best Technology for Escaping from a Submarine Is No Technology" (*American Heritage of Invention and Technology,* Summer 1986), pp. 44–49.

42. "Loss of the U.S.S. *Tang*," p. 254.

43. Caverly, oral history, University of Minnesota.

44. Caverly, interview with the author.

45. Leibold, interview with the author.

46. Ibid.

47. *New York Times*, September 1, 1945.

48. Leibold, letter to the author.

49. Caverly, oral history, University of Minnesota.

50. "Loss of the U.S.S. *Tang*," p. 252.

51. Larry Savadkin, interview with the author.

52. DaSilva, written account of his time aboard the *Tang*.

53. Pete Narowanski later maintained that he raised his arm in the air to indicate his position and the Japanese shot him through the wrist. Morris.

54. "Loss of the U.S.S. *Tang*," p. 254.

55. Decker.

56. In an official report on the escape, another of the survivors recalled seeing Larson's body on the deck of the P-34. The Japanese were kicking and slapping him to try to revive him, but without success. "Loss of the U.S.S. *Tang*," p. 254.

57. Adams.

58. O'Kane, p. 19.

Chapter 10

1. Floyd Caverly, interview with the author.

2. Caverly, oral history, University of Minnesota.

3. Caverly, Leibold, and O'Kane had been in the water for about eight hours when they were picked up. "There had been nine men on the bridge when the *Tang* went down," recalled Leibold. "Three of us had stayed afloat and the other six had drowned."

4. William Leibold, interview with the author.

5. Ibid.

6. Clay Decker, oral history, Regis University.

7. Larry Savadkin, "Saga of POWs" (*All Hands*, June 1946).

8 Decker.

9. Caverly, interview with the author.

10. Ibid.

11. Ibid.

12. Jesse DaSilva, written account of his time aboard the *Tang*.

13. Leibold.

14. Ibid.

15. Richard O'Kane, *Clear the Bridge!* (New York: Ballantine Books, 1977), p. 285.

16. Savadkin.

17. Leibold.

18. O'Kane, p. 460.

19. Leibold.

20. DaSilva.

21. Savadkin.

22. Leibold.

23. Savadkin.

24. Leibold.

25. Ibid.

26. O'Kane, p. 462.

27. Leibold.

28. Ibid.

29. O'Kane, p. 462.

30. William Tuohy, *The Bravest Man* (Stroud, England: Sutton Publishing, 2001), p. 340.

Chapter 11

1. Cindy Adams, "USS *Tang* Survivors" (*Polaris,* February 1981).

2. Richard O'Kane, *Clear the Bridge!* (New York: Ballantine Books, 1977), pp. 462–463.

3. *Wall Street Journal,* April 7, 2005.

4. Jesse DaSilva, oral history, Indiana Historical Society.

5. http://www.acepilopts.com/usmc_boyington.html.

6. William Leibold, letter to the author.

7. Clay Decker, oral history, Regis University.

8. George Brown, oral history, personal files of George Rocek.

9. O'Kane, pp. 462–463.

10. Adams.

11. O'Kane, pp. 462–463.

12. Chuck Ver Valin, interview with the author.

13. Charles A. Lockwood, *Sink 'em All* (New York: Bantam Books, 1984), p. 351.

14. Floyd Caverly, interview with the author.

15. Adams.

16. O'Kane, pp. 462–463.

17. Decker.

18. DaSilva, written account of his time aboard the *Tang*.

19. Caverly.

20. The *Tang* survivors quickly learned how to warn each other about that day's subject of inquiry. Ibid.

21. Larry Savadkin, "Saga of POWs" (*All Hands*, June 1946).

22. Ibid.

23. Caverly.

24. Adams.

25. DaSilva, written account of his time aboard the *Tang*.

26. Leibold, interview with the author.

27. Caverly.

28. Ibid.

29. Ibid.

30. Leibold, letter to the author.

31. O'Kane, p. 464.

32. Murray Frazee, interview with the author.

33. James F. DeRose, *Unrestricted Warfare* (New York: John Wiley & Sons, 2000), p. 226.

34. Leibold, interview with the author.

35. Joyce Paul, e-mail to the author.

36. Jackie Morris, interview with the author.

37. William Tuohy, *The Bravest Man* (Stroud, England: Sutton Publishing, 2001), pp. 362–363.

38. Ibid., p. 363.

39. DeRose, p. 292.

40. Adams.

41. Report of Recovery Team No. 56, HQ Amer. Div. Arty APO 716, September 22, 1945.

42. Caverly.

43. Ibid.

44. Ibid.

45. Barbara Lane, interview with the author.

Chapter 12

1. Richard O'Kane, *Clear the Bridge!* (New York: Ballantine Books, 1977), p. 464.

2. "We only received three of these boxes and we got the third one only because Commander O'Kane was able to persuade the guards to give it to us," recalled Jesse DaSilva. "They had more but we figured they kept them for themselves." Cindy Adams, "USS *Tang* Survivors" (*Polaris*, February 1981).

3. Hervie Haufler, *Codebreakers' Victory* (New York: New American Library, 2003), p. 220.

4. In no small part, the sinkings had been made possible by the superb intelligence provided to O'Kane and his fellow captains by naval intelligence. As Vice Admiral Charles Lockwood put it: "During periods, which fortunately were brief, when enemy code changes temporarily cut off supply of Communication Intelligence, its absence was keenly felt. The curve of enemy contacts and of consequent sinkings almost exactly paralleled the curve of Communication Intelligence available." Ibid.

5. O'Kane, p. 464.

6. Report of Recovery Team No. 56, HQ Amer. Div. Arty APO 716, 22 September 1945.

7. James DeRose, *Unrestricted Warfare* (New York: John Wiley & Sons, 2000), p. 253.

8. William Leibold, interview with the author.

9. Report of Recovery Team No. 56.

10. D. F. Weiss, Commander U.S. Navy, letter to Mrs. Floyd Caverly, February 6, 1945.

11. O'Kane, p. 465.

12. Leibold, letter to the author.

13. Jesse DaSilva, written account of his time aboard the *Tang*.

14. O'Kane, p. 465.

15. Ibid.

16. Bruce Gamble, *Black Sheep One* (New York: Ballantine Books, 2000), p. 365.

17. Louis Zamperini, *Devil at My Heels* (New York: Harper Collins, 2003), p. 153.

Chapter 13

1. Jesse DaSilva, written account of his time aboard the *Tang*.

2. Ibid.

3. Caverly, interview with the author.

4. Clay Decker, oral history, Regis University.

5. Floyd Caverly, interview with the author.

6. Ibid.

7. Bruce Gamble, *Black Sheep One* (New York: Ballantine Books, 2000), p. 366.

8. Cindy Adams, "USS *Tang* Survivors" (*Polaris*, February 1981).

9. Gavan Daws, *Prisoners of the Japanese* (New York: William Morrow, 1994), p. 322.

10. Pappy Boyington was a chronic smoker. As he and the *Tang* veterans cleared their way through rubble, he scoured the ground for cigarette butts. Back in the cell he shared with Decker, he would take a small lens he had obtained secretly and wait until

NOTES TO CHAPTER 14

the sun reached the exact position where it shone into his cell. "He'd roll that tobacco in a [Japanese bank note] and get up there at the window with his mouth on one end and I'd hold the lens and he'd get it lit. Then he'd chain-smoke all of the cigarettes he had because the sun would change position and I couldn't light another one." Clay Decker, oral history, Regis University.

11. The army guards at Omori were not as sadistic as the guards at Ofuna but they did dole out fierce beatings if they felt like it. One of the more vicious guards, known as "Horseface" to the inmates because he had thick lips and buck teeth, was in command of the *Tang* survivors when they had to leave the camp on work details. One day, he beat Larry Savadkin, hitting him with a pair of pliers. Floyd Caverly recalled: "There was blood running down his face . . ." Adams.

12. Ibid.

13. Ibid.

14. James F. DeRose, *Unrestricted Warfare* (New York: John Wiley & Sons, 2000), p. 253.

Chapter 14

1. Gregory Boyington, *Baa Baa Black Sheep* (New York: Bantam Books, 1987), p. 301.

2. Edwin P. Hoyt, *Japan's War* (New York: McGraw-Hill Book Company, 1986), p. 438.

3. Richard O'Kane, *Clear the Bridge!* (New York: Ballantine Books, 1977), p. 466.

4. Ibid.

5. Boyington, p. 308.

6. Gavan Daws, *Prisoners of the Japanese, POWs of WWII in the Pacific* (New York: William Morrow, 1994), p. 337.

7. O'Kane, p. 466.

8. Jesse DaSilva, written account of his time aboard the *Tang*.

9. Boyington, p. 311.

10. Daws, p. 343.

11. Boyington, p. 312.

12. Robert Goldsworthy, oral history, Washington State oral history program.

13. Cindy Adams, "USS *Tang* Survivors" (*Polaris*, February 1981).

14. Floyd Caverly, interview with the author.

15. Marsha Allen, interview with the author.

16. Gavan Daws, *Prisoners of the Japanese* (New York: William Morrow, 1994), p. 343.

17. Jesse DaSilva was also taken aboard the hospital ship *Benevolence*. He was the only one of the survivors who was not flown home. Instead he spent three weeks at sea.

18. Saylor, p. 225.

19. "Survivors' Battle Adds to *Tang*'s Epic," *New York Times*, September 1, 1945.

Chapter 15

1. Dan Van der Vat, *The Pacific Campaign* (New York: Simon and Schuster, 1991), pp. 400–401.

2. James DeRose, *Unrestricted Warfare* (New York: John Wiley & Sons, 2000), p. 259.

3. Ernestine O'Kane to families of the *Tang*'s crew, September 2, 1945.

4. Charles A. Lockwood, *Sink 'em All* (New York: Bantam, 1984), p. 347.

5. "We organized a regular detail of officers and stenographers

to interview each man and record their stories," recalled Lock-wood. "I talked to as many as I could and was shocked to observe the shifty, hunted look in their eyes and the punch-drunk condition of many. Some, I feared, would never be quite normal again. All data collected was sent to the Office of Naval Intelligence in the hope that it could be used in the trials of war criminals." Ibid.

6. William Leibold, interview with the author.

7. Floyd Caverly, interview with the author.

8. Ibid.

9. Ibid.

10. Leibold.

11. Ibid.

12. *Los Angeles Times*, September 1, 1945.

13. Leibold.

14. *Los Angeles Daily News*, August 31, 1945.

15. Richard O'Kane, *Clear the Bridge!* (New York: Ballantine Books, 1977), p. 464.

16. "POWs from Japan Reach U.S.," *Associated Press*, September 7, 1945.

17. William Tuohy, *The Bravest Man* (Stroud, England: Sutton Publishing, 2001), p. 393.

18. Clay Decker, oral history, Regis University.

19. Ibid.

20. Ibid.

21. Leibold.

22. Barbara Lane, interview with the author.

23. Joyce DaSilva, interview with the author.

24. Lane.

25. Leibold.

26. DeRose, p. 263.

27. Caverly.

Chapter 16

1. Medal of Honor Citation of Commander Richard Hetherington O'Kane: "For conspicuous gallantry and intrepidity at the risk of his life above and beyond the call of duty as Commanding Officer of the USS TANG operating against two enemy Japanese convoys on October 23 and 24, 1944, during her Fifth and last War Patrol. Boldly maneuvering on the surface into the midst of a heavily escorted convoy, Commander O'Kane stood in a fusillade of bullets and shells from all directions to launch smashing hits on three tankers, coolly swung his ship to fire at a freighter and, in a split second decision, shot out of the path of an onrushing transport, missing it by inches. Boxed in by blazing tankers, a freighter, transport and several destroyers, he blasted two of the targets with his remaining torpedoes and, with pyrotechnics bursting on all sides, cleared the area. Twenty-four hours later, he again made contact with a heavily escorted convoy steaming to support the Leyte campaign with reinforcements and supplies and with crated planes piled high on each unit. In defiance of the enemy's relentless fire, he closed the concentration of ships and in quick succession sent two torpedoes each into the first and second transports and an adjacent tanker, finding his mark with each torpedo in a series of violent explosions at less than a thousand-yard range. With ships bearing down from all sides, he charged the enemy at high speed, exploding the tanker in a burst of flame, smashing the transport dead in the water and blasting the destroyer with a mighty roar which rocked the TANG from stem to stern. Expending his last two torpedoes into the remnants of a once powerful convoy before his own ship went down, Commander O'Kane, aided by his gallant command, achieved an illustrious record of heroism in combat, enhancing the finest traditions of the United States Naval Service."

2. William Tuohy, *The Bravest Man* (Stroud, England: Sutton Publishing, 2001), p. 396.

3. William Leibold, interview with the author.

4. Floyd Caverly, interview with the author.

5. Leibold.

6. Bill Gallagher, letter to Jesse DaSilva.

7. Leibold.

8. Caverly.

9. Leibold.

10. Caverly.

11. http://warfish.com/gaz_tangmem.html.

12. Leibold.

13. http://www.arlingtoncemetery.net/rokane.htm.

14. Ibid.

15. Ibid.

16. Edward L. Beach, *Submarine!* (Annapolis, Maryland: Bluejacket Books, 2003), p. 151.

17. Tuohy, p. 23.

18. Jackie Morris, interview with the author.

19. Ibid.

20. Floyd Caverly, interview with the author.

21. Pimlico race results, courtesy of Jackie Morris.

22. Morris.

23. Jesse DaSilva, interview with Douglas E. Clanin. Oral history, Indiana Historical Society.

24. Ibid.

25. Ibid.

26. Joyce Paul, letter to the author.

27. Ibid.

28. *USA Today*, August 16, 2000.

29. Clay Decker, oral history, Regis University.

30. *Sabalo* Memoirs of Lt. Robert C. Bell Jr. http://uss sabalo.org/T-BellMemoirs.htm.

31. Barbara Lane, interview with the author.

32. Caverly.

33. Ibid.

34. Thomas Saylor, *Long Hard Road: American POWs During WW II* (St. Paul, Minnesota: Minnesota Historical Society Press, 2007), p. 91.

35. Marsha Allen, interview with the author.

BIBLIOGRAPHY

Alden, John Doughty. *U.S. Submarine Attacks During World War II*. Annapolis, Md.: U.S. Naval Institute, 1989.

Beach, Edward Latimer. *Run Silent Run Deep*. London: Cassell, 2003.

———. *Submarine!* Annapolis, Md: Bluejacket Books, 2003.

Blair, Clay. *Silent Victory*. Annapolis, Md: Naval Institute Press, 2001.

Boyington, Gregory. *Baa, Baa, Black Sheep*. New York: Bantam Books, 1987.

Calvert, James F. *Silent Running*. New York: John Wiley & Sons, 1995.

Chambliss, William C. *The Silent Service*. New York: New American Library, Signet Books, 1959.

Compton-Hall, Richard. *The Underwater War: 1939–1945*. Poole, Dorset, England: Blandford Press, 1982.

Daws, Gavan. *Prisoners of the Japanese*. New York: William Morrow, 1994.

DeRose, James. *Unrestricted Warfare: How a New Breed of Officers Led the Submarine Force to Victory in World War II*. New York: John Wiley & Sons, 2000.

Edwards, Bernard. *Blood and Bushido*. New York: Brick Tower Press, 1991.

Fluckey, Eugene Bennett. *Thunder Below*. Urbana, Ill.:
  University of Illinois Press, 1992.
Galantin, Ignatius Joseph. *Take Her Deep*. Chapel Hill, N.C.:
  Algonquin Books, 1987.
Gamble, Bruce. *Black Sheep One*. New York: Ballantine Books,
  2000.
Glusman, John. *Conduct Under Fire*. New York: Viking, 2005.
Gray, Edwyn. *Few Survived: A History of Submarine Disasters*.
  London: Leo Cooper, 1986.
Grider, George William. *Warfish*. New York: Little, Brown, 1958.
Gugliotta, Bobette. *Pigboat 39: An American Sub Goes to War*.
  Lexington, Ky.: University Press of Kentucky, 1984.
Hara, Tameichi. *Japanese Destroyer Captain*. New York:
  Ballantine, 1961.
Haufler, Hervie, *Codebreakers' Victory*. New York: New American
  Library, 2003.
Holmes, W. J. *Double-Edged Secrets: U.S. Naval Intelligence
  Operations in the Pacific During World War II*. Annapolis,
  Md.: U.S. Naval Institute, 1979.
———. *Underseas Victory: The Influence of Submarine
  Operations in the Pacific in World War II*. New York:
  Doubleday, 1966.
Horton, Edward. *The Illustrated History of the Submarine*.
  London: Sidgwick & Jackson, 1974.
Hoyt, Edwin P. *Japan's War*. New York: McGraw-Hill Book
  Company, 1986.
———. *Submarines at War: The History of the American Silent
  Service*. New York: Stein & Day, 1983.
Keegan, John. *The Price of Admiralty*. London: Viking Penguin,
  1989.
Kimmet, Larry, and Margaret Regis. *U.S. Submarines in World*

War II: An Illustrated History. Seattle, Wash.: Navigator Publishing, 1996.

Lavo, Carl. *Back from the Deep.* Annapolis, Md.: U.S. Naval Institute, 1994.

Lockwood, Charles A. *Down to the Sea in Subs.* New York: W. W. Norton, 1967.

———. *Sink 'em All.* New York: Bantam Books, 1984.

———. *Through Hell and Deep Water.* Philadelphia: Childon, 1956.

Maas, Peter. *The Rescuer.* New York: Harper & Row, 1967.

Mason, John T., Jr. *The Pacific War Remembered.* Annapolis, Md.: U.S. Naval Institute, 1986.

McDaniel, J. T., ed. *USS Tang (SS-306) American Submarine War Patrol Reports,* Ga.: Riverdale Books, 2005.

Mendenhall, Corwin. *Submarine Diary.* Chapel Hill, N.C.: Algonquin Books, 1991.

Miller, David. *Submarines of the World.* New York: Salamander Books, 1991.

Miller, Nathan. *War at Sea.* Oxford, England: Oxford University Press, 1995.

Morison, Samuel Eliot. *The Two-Ocean War: A Short History of the United States Navy in the Second World War.* Boston: Little, Brown, 1963.

Navy Times editors. *They Fought Under the Sea.* Harrisburg, Pa.: Stackpole, 1962.

O'Kane, Richard H. *Clear the Bridge! The War Patrols of the USS Tang.* New York: Ballantine Books, 1977.

———. *Wahoo: The Patrols of America's Most Famous World War II Submarine.* Novato, Calif.: Presidio Press, 1987.

Padfield, Peter. *War Beneath the Sea: Submarine Conflict 1939–1945.* London: John Murray, 1995.

Parrish, Thomas. *The Submarine.* New York: Viking, 2004.

Polmar, Norman. *The Naval Institute Guide to the Ships and Aircraft of the U.S. Fleet.* Annapolis, Md.: U.S. Naval Institute, 1965.

Roscoe, Theodore. *U.S. Submarine Operations in World War II.* Annapolis, Md.: U.S. Naval Institute, 1949.

Saylor, Thomas. *Long Hard Road, American POWs During WW II.* Minn.: Minnesota Historical Society Press, 2007.

Shelford, W. O. *Subsunk.* New York: Doubleday, 1960.

Sterling, Forest J. *Wake of the Wahoo.* Chapel Hill, N.C.: Professional Press, 1997.

Stern, Robert C. *U.S. Subs in Action.* Carrollton, Tex.: Squadron/Signal Publications, 1983.

Tuohy, William. *The Bravest Man: The Story of Richard O'Kane & U.S. Submariners in the Pacific War.* Stroud, England: Sutton Publishing, 2001.

U.S. Naval Historical Division. *The Submarine in the United States Navy.* Washington, D.C.: 1969.

———. *U.S. Submarine Losses in World War II.* Washington, D.C.: 1963.

Van der Vat, Dan. *Stealth at Sea: The History of the Submarine.* London: Orion, 1994.

———. *The Pacific Campaign.* New York: Simon & Schuster, 1991.

Walkowiak, Thomas F. *Fleet Submarines of World War II.* Missoula, Mont.: Pictorial Histories Publishing Company, 1988.

Werner, Herbert A. *Iron Coffins.* New York: Henry Holt and Company, 1969.

Wheeler, Keith. *War Under the Pacific.* New York: Time Life Books, 1980.

Winton, John. *Ultra in the Pacific: How Breaking Japanese Codes and Ciphers Affected Naval Operations Against Japan.* London: Leo Cooper, 1993.

Zamperini, Louis. *Devil at My Heels.* New York: Harper Collins, 2003.

INDEX

still and, 42
submarine activity (8/1944),
    5–10
torpedo circular run, 61–62,
    86, 146–147
trip to Formosa Strait, 32–38,
    41, 42
O'Kane, Ernestine
hope for husband's return,
    161, 177, 189
husband's love for, 76, 207
launching of USS O'Kane
    and, 209
Leibold and, 215
letter from Lockwood,
    162–163
message from Dornin, 177
Omori rescue news and, 188
reflections on husband, 209
survivor information and, 160
Tang wives and, 162, 194
Western Union telegram to,
    161–162
See also Groves, Ernestine
O'Kane, James, 76, 163
O'Kane, Marsha, 76, 163,
    215–216
Omori camp
bombing raids and, 174–175
description, 172, 173
news media and, 185–186,
    188

rescue/evacuation, 184–189
revenge and, 183
Omori camp/Tang survivors
after surrender, 181–184
beatings, 243n11
bombing raids and, 174–175
diet/effects, 174, 176–177,
    182, 187
drunken guards and,
    182–183
food dropped for, 183–184
health of, 173–174
rescue/evacuation, 184–189,
    243n18
as "special prisoners," 173,
    174, 175
transfer to, 171–172
work detail, 176–177,
    179–180

P-34, Japanese patrol boat, 130,
    131, 132, 133, 138, 142
P-50, Japanese ship, 132
Pearce, Basil
escape plan and, 111, 112,
    117–118
escape training, 234n1
Formosa Strait trip, 34
Pearl Harbor
1941 attack/consequences,
    31, 224n8
R and R at, 16